MOTORCYCLE JOURNEYS THROUGH
BAJA

by Clement Salvadori

A Whirlaway Book
Whitehorse Press
North Conway, New Hampshire

A Whirlaway Book. Published September 1997 by
    Whitehorse Press
    P.O. Box 60
    North Conway, New Hampshire 03860 U.S.A.
    Phone: 603-356-6556 or 800-531-1133
    FAX: 603-356-6590

Whirlaway and Whitehorse Press are trademarks of
Kennedy Associates.

ISBN 1-884313-08-6

5   4   3

Printed in the United States of America

GLASER

This book is dedicated to the P.M. of Cat Crossing

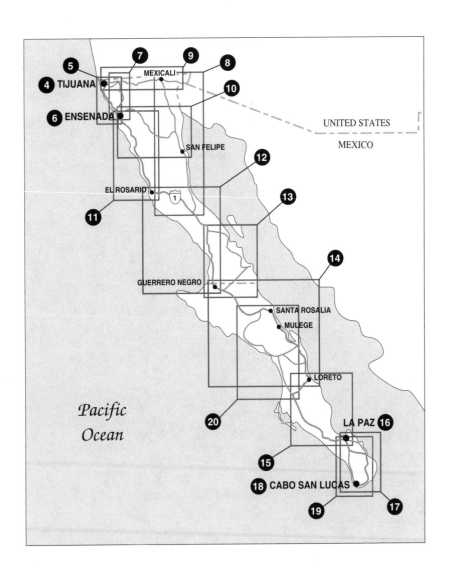

Contents

∙∙

Introduction

If I can presume that we are all sensible riders, I will presume
that we all begin at the beginning of this book, by reading the
Introduction.

This is the literary equivalent of my being introduced to
you: "Clement, I'd like you to meet Mr./Ms. Smith." "A
pleasure, I'm sure." We hope so.

How did I get to write this book? Dan Kennedy, the pub-
lisher of Whitehorse Press, called me up and asked me to
do it, promising wealth and fame as a reward for months of
hard work. In my vanity, I agreed.

Truth is, I have been motorcycling the through the Baja
for some years. I first traveled the entire peninsula in
March of 1975. Riding north from Panama, I had stopped
for the night in Puerto Vallarta, Mexico on the Mexican
mainland coast. Having been on the road for two years, I
wasn't really up on local events. I learned that there was a
ferry running from Vallarta up to the tip of Baja, Cabo San
Lucas, and that the road running the length of Baja had
been paved, and was now officially known as Mexico
Route 1, or the Transpeninsular Highway.

What a deal! And so I went, with only an old map of
Mexico to guide me. Not that I needed much guidance:
"Just follow the new asphalt for a thousand miles," advised
one motorhomer.

That Vallarta-Cabo ferry quit running a number of years
ago, but I've been going back to Baja ever since, and will
be back many more times. A little bit of the arcane knowledge I have gained over the years is now immortalized in
this book.

With this volume tucked in your tankbag, you can enter
the marvelous, mysterious peninsula of Baja California
without fear.

This guide to the pleasures of Baja California is intended for all manner of motorcyclists, whether on sport bikes, touring rigs, dual-purpose machines, or any other motorcycle which tends to follow established roads, be they four-lane divided highways or gnarly, narrow, dirt byways in the mountains. I do not address the wishes of the serious Baja-bashing off-roaders, but the person driving the dirt-donks' chase vehicle will appreciate the information herein. Whether you are riding a GL1500, a DR350, or something else with a license plate hanging off the back end, this is the book for you.

The book is user-friendly, highly informative, occasionally repetitive when deemed necessary, and—I trust—entertaining.

A small number of Spanish words have been included in italics, and are explained as you read along. To make reading easier, we have omitted all Spanish accents except for the ñ.

The table of contents lists 20 chapters with basic maps to cover all of the reasonable roads in Baja and four of the major cities. The chapter headings are quite clear: Want to know about the city of Cabo San Lucas? Look up Chapter 18. The road from Ensenada to Tecate? Chapter 7.

Life can be simple, and this guidebook supports that.

I would like to acknowledge the help I've gotten from my good friend Kurt Grife who has been a Baja hound since the early 1970s. We met in the Hacienda Hotel in Mulege one morning a dozen years ago, and he told me he wanted to ride, or drive, every single road in Baja. Since then, we've ridden to a lot of places in the back of beyond that I never would have gone to otherwise, for which I have *usually* thanked him (the other times I have cursed him).

This book will be updated every couple of years. If any readers find my information faulty or out of date, or come across new things they feel should be included, do let me know: 8240 Toloso Rd, Atascadero, CA 93422.

Indispensable Info

This road across the Vizcaino Desert climbs into the Sierra San Francisco to the village of San Francisco, near which are several caves with rock paintings from a vanished culture.

1 Where Are You Going?

· ·

A (Mercifully) Brief Geological, Historical, and Sociological Introduction to Baja California.

Lay out a map of North America and run a line from San Francisco Bay south-southeast down to the mouth of the **Sea of Cortez** (sometimes referred to as the Gulf of California), which separates Baja California from the rest of Mexico. You have just roughly traced the line of the infamous **San Andreas Fault,** which, if geologists are to be believed, split Baja from the mainland about 30 million years ago. Those who adhere to the teachings of Bishop Ussher, who maintained that the entire universe was created in 4004 B.C., are free to disagree.

That thick finger of land, 58,000 square miles, that juts southeastwardly for 800 miles, is not really blessed with much in the way of natural resources—at least not the kind that keep people alive. Although it had many scattered sources of spring water to satisfy the wild animals and early Indian inhabitants, it's essentially dry. Except, of course, when the rains come, and then there is often too much water. Every year or two a major storm blasts through some part of Baja and tears up everything, destroying roads and interrupting traffic. Unless you're camping in some remote spot without benefit of radio, however, you'll know when something big is coming. Just pay attention to the weather reports.

Three big mountain ranges, and a lot of little ones, cover most of the middle of the peninsula. In the north is the **Sierra Juarez,** in the middle is the **Sierra Giganta,** in the south is the **Sierra Laguna.** A big desert, the **Vizcaino,** sits on the 28th parallel, right at the junction of the two states that comprise Baja.

Political note: Mexico is officially known as the **United States of Mexico,** with 31 states and the Federal District of

Mexico City (like our District of Columbia). Baja was a territory until the state of **Baja California,** the northern half, was created in 1952; for clarification it is sometimes referred to, incorrectly, as Baja California Norte. Twenty-two years later, just after the completion of the Carreteria Transpeninsula, **Baja California Sur** became the 31st state.

Mexico Route 1 is known as the **Transpeninsular Highway,** 1,060 miles of asphalt running from Tijuana in the north to Cabo San Lucas in the south. Without that highway, this book would not have been written.

Baja has been inhabited for more than 1,000 years, but the only sign of the earliest inhabitants are the many cave paintings they left behind. The **Indians** who came after, and who greeted the Spaniards (sometimes with open arms, sometimes with arrows) claimed no relationship to the cave painters.

History, as preserved by the written word, began in 1534 when a Spanish ship sailed into the Bay of La Paz. Twenty-three of the crew were killed by Indians while seeking water; the rest sensibly sailed away.

Various explorers sailed up and down the coast, occasionally landing, for the next 150 years, but the first permanent **Spanish** presence did not occur until 1697, when the Jesuits founded a mission in Loreto. They brought not only their strange god, but also strange diseases against which the Indians had no defenses.

In 1734, the southern Indians revolted and did in a few missionaries to celebrate the bicentennial of their first effort to keep the Europeans out. A hundred troops came and restored order.

By the early 1800s, mainland Mexicans were dissatisfied with the rule of Spain and with the wealthy Catholic Church. By 1821 the colonials were in open revolt against Spain. Baja was declared a territory of the **Mexican Republic** in 1824.

After the Spanish left, the **Catholic Church** (which had not backed the revolutionary colonialists) found its power, and its financial position, eroded. In 1857 President Benito Juarez (many streets are named after him) altered the constitution to force the Catholic Church to sell all its secular

The mission at San Ignacio was built by the Jesuits in 1728, rebuilt by the Dominicans in 1786, and restored with the help of the Mexican government in 1976.

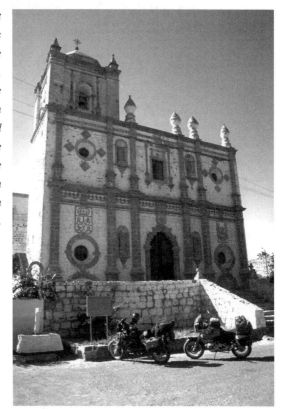

When in Rome . . .

Most Mexicans are quite Catholic and quite religious, attending Sunday services whenever possible. Whether you seek spiritual comfort or just wish to to appreciate the local mores, you would be welcome at any church, as long as you act and dress appropriately: be quiet and respectful, wear long pants, and women should also have their arms covered, and preferably a scarf on their heads. Should you be at a far-removed place like Mission Borja when a priest is delivering a sermon, I do recommend you attend; it will be a memorable time. Your motorcycle garb would be perfectly acceptable, because everyone will know you came by bike and probably did not have a white shirt in your bags.

■

California is named after the legendary Queen Calafia, from the 16th century Spanish novel The Adventures of Esplandian; *this portrait of her on her winged gryphon hangs in the Calafia Ocean Resort.*

property—it could keep the churches. If you wonder why you don't see any white-collar clerics or black-cassocked *padres* in the the city streets today, it is because they are still forbidden by law from leaving church grounds in religious garb. The clergy are out and about, but in chinos and plaid shirts.

In 1846 and 1847, during the **Mexican American War,** U.S. troops made a few forays into Baja. In 1848 the **Treaty of Guadalupe Hidalgo** ceded Alta California (along with Texas and a few other places) to the Americans, and the California/Mexico border was drawn one league south of the entrance to San Diego Bay, going due east to the Colorado River.

By the 1880s, only half a dozen mission fathers (Dominican) were left in all of Baja, and the population of the entire peninsula numbered less than 50,000. In an effort to make a little money off the place, the Mexican government actively pursued **foreign investment** in Baja, and was willing to lease, or even sell, land to foreigners.

The 20th century **Mexican Revolution** began in 1910, pitting the landless poor against the rich. In 1917, the government announced the *ejido,* or **Common Land Act.** which took land from the plutocrats and gave it back to the people. Roughly 70 percent of Baja became owned by the mixed-blood (mostly Indian and Spanish) *mestizos* who lived there.

You will see signs for Ejido Uruapan, Ejido Bonfil, hundreds of *ejidos*. These are all little communal villages, mostly agricultural, which have, at most, a *tienda* (store). One of the greatest problems faced by present day *norteamericanos* who wish to live or build a business in Baja is dealing with *ejido* land. The arrangements for dealing with an *ejido* are often arcane, and on more than one occasion, *ejido* authorities have reclaimed houses and even hotels built by foreigners.

Outside of the tourist zones, Bajaeños tend to be quiet and friendly. In the back country I have always been treated with the utmost courtesy when stopping to ask for directions or water. The tourist meccas in the north and south of Baja are fun, but the real pleasure of Baja is, for me, to be found in the hundreds of miles in between.

The dirt road to San Borja Mission goes through countryside populated only by various members of the cactus family.

A tire-repair kit, and the knowledge to use it, is highly advisable for anyone leaving the paved roads.

2 General Stuff to Know

∙∙

Common sense. Don't leave home without it. I remain bemused by the fact that a lot of people think anything goes once they are outside of the United States and safely on the foreign soil of Baja California. This unfortunate attitude is most apparent in the Tourist Zone in the north, and the Cabo Corridor in the south.

The truth is, once outside the U.S. you should be *more* polite, *more* considerate, and *more* careful. Common sense also dictates that you have a motorcycle in good condition and tires with a lot of wear left.

Money. Money is good. Dollars are good. *Pesos* are good. The current rate of exchange (8/97) is approaching eight *pesos* to one dollar, but it fluctuates. In the tourist zones, dollars are always acceptable; in between, it is useful to have *pesos*. If you go into a *tienda* to buy a bottle of water, *pesos* will be a better medium of exhange than greenbacks. Also, gas station attendants might well offer a lower rate of exchange than you can get at a bank, which gives them a little added profit.

In the tourist zones money-changers are everywhere. Outside of a T.Z. you might have to use banks, which are open only from 9:30 to 1:30, or thereabouts, Monday through Friday. Often the foreign-exchange window closes by noon, and lines can be long.

The plastic-money world is still in its infancy in Baja, although some Mexican ATMs will accept U.S. cards. Cash advances on your mainstream credit cards can usually be arranged from inside a bank. Travelers checks are easily negotiable in the bigger towns, and definitely in the T.Z.s. Credit cards are accepted in the tourist zones, and at many of the middling to better hotels in between, but cash is king.

Paperwork. Though a weekend joy ride down to Ensenada requires nothing in the way of ID, it is useful to have proof of who you are, just in case. A U.S. driver's license will suffice, but you might carry a passport or a notarized copy of your birth certificate as backup.

If you happen to lose your wallet, with every bit of identification inside, you can head either for the border or the nearest U.S. Consulate. Chances are you won't ever be required to show any ID at any time, but it is handy to have along, especially if you happen to imbibe too much tequila and wake up in the morning not quite sure of who you are.

Mexican legal protocol requires that you have a Tourist Card if you are going to be in Baja more than 72 hours, or are traveling south of Ensenada. I have never been asked to show mine, but I always have it, appropriately filled in and officially stamped. These TCs are available at any border crossing, and should be stamped there as well.

For the motorcycle, you'll need to carry your registration and a copy of your title. If you are going to take a ferry over to the Mexican mainland, proper and extensive paperwork for the bike is essential: you must have a Tourist Card, proof of ownership of the vehicle, and a Temporary Vehicle Import Permit. These will be checked at the boat. You will also need a credit card.

Proof of ownership requires original documents, nothing that is photocopied. It is a hassle, but this is what is required . . . and don't say I didn't tell you. If your name is not on the ownership document, you will need notarized authorization from the legal owner; life is a whole lot easier, however, if the name on all the documents is the same.

The Temporary Vehicle Import Permit ($11) provides the Mexican government with a guarantee that you will re-export the motorcycle from mainland Mexico. At one time it was popular for *norteamericanos* to drive deep down into Mexico, have a good time, sell their vehicle for a small profit, and fly/train/bus home. The Mexican bureaucrats want to make sure they get their tax cut these days.

If you want to get a TVIP before leaving home, your AAA club can help, or you can contact the nearest Mexican Tourist Office, of which there are at least five: Washington DC, 202-659-8730; New York City, 212-755-7261; Chicago, 312-565-2786: Houston, 713-880-5153; Los Angeles, 213-203-8151 or 800-262-8900.

Insurance. The Mexican auto insurance industry has a great scam working: your U.S. insurance company cannot cover you in Mexico. All around any border crossing, well-advertised agents will sell you a policy for a day or more. You should have liability insurance, just in case. According to Mexican law, if you are in an accident and cannot produce proof of liability insurance, whether you are right or wrong, it's off to the slammer you go. Current liability rates are about $7 a day, a bit less for longer policies.

At least one company, Instant Mexico Auto Insurance Services (phone U.S. 800-345-4701), will also cover your motorcycle for fire, theft, and collision with a $1,000 deductible. There may be others I'm not aware of. IMAIS offices are at the San Ysidro Avenue exit from I-5, at 223 Via de San Ysidro. They can also fax you a policy.

There are also two Baja motor clubs, mostly geared to motorhomers: the Discover Baja Travel Club (phone U.S. 800-727-BAJA), and the Club Vagabundos del Mar (phone U.S. 800-474-BAJA). Both are headquartered near San Diego. It may cost a fair bit to join, but these clubs can provide less expensive liability insurance. Calling up to get their information packets is worthwhile.

Legal Issues. Should you run afoul of the law, tell the police you must get in touch with a U.S. Consular Officer, either in Cabo San Lucas (phone 33536 or 33566) or Ti-

Since your U.S. insurance is not valid in Mexico, it makes sense to buy some Mexican insurance when you go to Baja.

juana (phone 81-7400, after hours 619-585-2000). One of
the consul's less savory jobs is to look after American citizens who have been busted. Of course, if your transgres-
sion is minor, you could try to bribe your way out of
difficulty by offering a *mordida*—literally translated as "a
bite," because the official has taken a "bite" out of you.
However, my lawyer says I risk liability if I recommend
such a practice, so I don't. But, others have told me this can
be a quick way out of small problems. I disapprove of the
practice of *mordidas*, as the local constabulary might come
to look on this shakedown as an acceptable way to improve
their finances.

On an added note, I do not worry much about crime in
Baja; in the Tourist Zones there are occasional pickpockets
and purses-snatchers, but sensible precautions keep these
types at bay. If something untoward does happen, and you
are staying at a hotel, let the desk clerk help you get in
touch with the authorities. Or just find the nearest police-
man yourself.

The Baja *bandito* is mostly the stuff of legend. And everybody knows that if a *gringo* is too poor to own a car, and
can only afford a motorcycle, he is not worth robbing.

Gas. Don't worry about gas unless you're running
some highly tweaked, 100-octane motor. Gas is a state mo-
nopoly. All gas stations are called PEMEX *(PEtroleos MEXicanos)*. You will generally see a blue pump and a green
pump. The blue is regular leaded, with an advertised octane
rating of 80. You'll want the unleaded green pump (*Magna
Sin*), which claims 92 octane; I think the octane rating is a
bit on the optimistic side, but I have run all manner of modern bikes, from Harleys to HYKS (standing for Honda,
Yamaha, Kawasaki, Suzuki, creating an acronym pronounced "hicks"), BMWs and Triumphs on *Magna Sin,*
and never had a problem. Gas is sold in liters, not gallons,
with roughly four liters (3.7854, to be precise) to the gallon.

On the main roads, the only lack of PEMEX stations
might be on the 200 miles of Mexico 1 between El Rosario
and Villa Jesus Maria. As you'll learn in Chapter 12, there
are ways around that if you don't have a 200-mile tank. On
the dirt roads it is another matter, but any passing vehicle is

Gas is where you find it; this little station is in the village of La Purisima.

a source of fuel. As a matter of course, I always carry a small siphoning gadget with me—just in case.

Getting to the border. Get a map of California. The most used border crossing is the 24-hour border at San Ysidro, on Interstate 5 south of San Diego. That crossing is good for going to Tijuana or Ensenada.

The second border crossing is about five miles east on the Otay Mesa, which puts you in the industrial section of east Tijuana near the Tijuana Airport. The way to Otay Mesa is clearly marked on I-5, but unless you want to take Mexico 2-D to Tecate, there is not much sense in using this crossing. Also, Otay Mesa is closed from 10 p.m. to 6 a.m.

The third crossing is at Tecate. Pick up California Highway 94 from I-5 as it passes through San Diego, go 42 miles east, and there you are. The Tecate crossing is closed from midnight to 6 a.m., and is usually very lightly trafficked. It is definitely the best exit to use when leaving Baja.

The fourth crossing (open 24 hours) is at Calexico/Mexicali, about 120 miles east of the Pacific. To get there you can take Interstate 8 from either San Diego or Arizona to El Centro, and California 111 south to Calexico. Most people using this entry are headed for San Felipe.

Should you be coming from the east, there is one other entry from California to Baja at Andrade/Algodones, right by the Colorado River. Take California 186 south from I-8, and there you are—but it is closed from 8 p.m. to 6 a.m.

Farther east, via Arizona and the Mexican state of Sonora, there are two more possible entries without the restrictions on riding into mainland Mexico. Coming west from Tucson you can take Arizona 86 to Why, and go south on Arizona 85 through Organ Pipe Cactus National Monument to the Lukeville/Sonoita crossing (open from 6 a.m. to 10 p.m.). From there you'd pick up Mexico Highway 2 going west for 165 miles to Mexicali; if you try to go east you will run into a checkpoint where you'll be asked to show your paperwork.

The second Arizona crossing is via Yuma, on I-8. Take the U.S. 95 exit off of I-8 and follow it south to the San Luis Arizona/San Luis Rio Colorado crossing. From there it is 40 miles west on Mexico 2 to Mexicali.

Helmet laws.   Both states in Baja California have helmet laws. Enforcement is entirely arbitrary. One day in

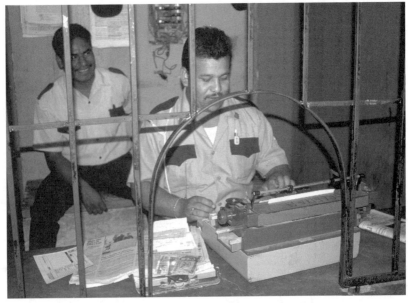

If you ride without a helmet in Cabo San Lucas, you just may get to pay a 35-peso ($6) fine to the authorities.

Cabo San Lucas, riding with the wind coursing over my bald spot, I was stopped, escorted to the police station, charged a *35-peso* fine, and sent on my way—without a helmet.

Weather.   When is the best time to go to Baja? Just about anytime, I would say, but best in spring and fall. The Pacific side generally stays cool, even in summer, thanks to the ocean air. On the other side of the peninsula, the Sea of Cortez is balmy from the end of September to the beginning of June, but damned hot during the summer. Of course, an odd tropical storm or hurricane can come in at any time, but that's just the luck of the draw; long-range forecasters usually have these plotted a week or more in advance. Between May and November, the infamous *chubascos* occasionally rip in and deluge the southern tip near Cabo for an hour or a week.

Telephones.   Many stores and restaurants all over Baja have phones which say DIAL THE U.S. DIRECT. Watch out for these, as they are a minor rip-off, charging some $25 for the convenience. If you wish to call home from Baja, use a telephone calling card, like Sprint or AT&T, and dial your card company's toll-free number.

If you want to call from the U.S. to the Hotel Perla in La Paz, dial 011 (the international dialing code), then 52 for Mexico (the country code), then 112 for La Paz (the area/city code), then 20777 to reach the Hotel Perla. To call from Loreto to La Paz, dial 91 (that gets you into the intercity line) 112 (area code) 20777. If you are in La Paz, just dial 20777.

Post Offices.   All cities and towns have *correos,* and the cost of sending a postcard to the U.S. is four *pesos,* a letter, five *pesos.* Many hotels sell stamps at the front desk, but you should stick them on yourself. Chances are about 99.9 to 1 that you will beat the *correos mexicanos* back to the destination you have on the address.

This chapter has been a primer on general stuff; at the back of the book are five appendices, with more information—everything from what to put in your tool kit to health concerns, et cetera.

If you wish to go the very low-bucks option in La Paz, the Hotel Yeneka is the place for you.

3 Miles, Roads, & Hotels

This is a brief explanation of the information in this book. It should get you just about anywhere in Baja, within roadable reason, and provide you with a place to stay.

Mileage logs. Each section of the Baja highways is dealt with separately in segments that make sense: Tijuana to Ensenada, Ensenada to Guerrero Negro, Guerrero Negro to Loreto, and all the rest.

I describe all the main roads, so if you just want to do the Tourist Quadrilateral in northern Baja—Tijuana-Ensenada-San Felipe-Mexicali—all those roads are covered. If you want to do a simple TJ to Cabo and back, that's covered. And, if you want to branch out a bit onto some major dirt roads, a couple of them are included, too.

I also do four cityscapes: Tijuana, Ensenada, La Paz, and Cabo San Lucas. These provide a more or less meaningful insight into these urban areas.

Reset your tripmeter to Mile 0 to start any given stretch. I have not attempted to be precise to tenths of miles, as speedometer error (including mine) does not make that practical. However, all the mileage notations are quite obvious, and if you don't see the road, the monument, the restaurant, or the PEMEX that I am talking about, have your eyes checked. We will be dealing in miles, but Mexican signage uses kilometers. A kilometer is roughly 5/8ths of a mile (0.62137 mile = 1 km). When I see a kilometer sign, like 120, I divide that by 8 (= 15) and multiply by 5, to get 75 miles, or close enough.

Read about your ride that day during breakfast, then stuff this book in your tankbag.

Roads. One rider's okay road is another rider's bad road. There is no objective way for riders to determine how good they are, and a lot of poor riders have inflated opinions of their motorcycle skills.

Map Key

The maps in this book use these easily recognized symbols:

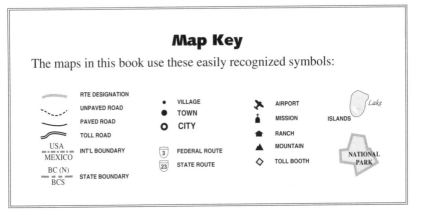

RTE DESIGNATION
UNPAVED ROAD
PAVED ROAD
TOLL ROAD
USA / MEXICO — INT'L BOUNDARY
BC (N) / BCS — STATE BOUNDARY

• VILLAGE
● TOWN
○ CITY
③ FEDERAL ROUTE
㉓ STATE ROUTE

✈ AIRPORT
⚑ MISSION
🏠 RANCH
▲ MOUNTAIN
◇ TOLL BOOTH

ISLANDS   *Lake*
NATIONAL PARK

I can only recommend that you come visit me, and if you feel comfortable riding down my driveway, 200 yards of crushed rock, I'll figure you're okay.

Riding in Baja is not like riding in the U.S. of A. You can do a nice trip to Cabo and never leave pavement—but things are a little *different* down south of the border.

First, while all pavement is pavement, good or bad, Baja pavement can change from a smooth 100-mph surface to shock-busters in a hundred yards. The paved roads are usually in acceptable shape, but you might run into a stretch that has more potholes than asphalt. So slow down.

Second, the paved roads generally do not have what we think of as shoulders. And there might be a five-inch drop off the asphalt to the dirt beside the road . . . and that might head steeply down into a ditch. The asphalt gets this thick because they just layer it up when redoing a road, and worry not a whit about the edges. A lot of informal dirt parking areas are beside the road where trucks pull off to stop. If you take advantage of these spots, you might have to negotiate those five inches of asphalt to get back on the highway. It's not hard to do, as long as you approach the situation with the throttle on.

Third, roads are often narrow, and sometimes oncoming big trucks or *norteamericano* motorhomes take up most of the pavement. Always stay to your side when going around a corner. Remember, there are usually no shoulders to escape onto.

Fourth, *pay attention* to road signs (see Appendix 6). Diamond-shaped signs mean something hazardous is ahead. The two most common problems are *vados* (dips) and *topes* (speed bumps). Usually these are sign-posted beforehand—but not always. The town of Maneadero is nicknamed Tope City. Only about half are marked.

Hitting a dip at speed can create some serious problems as you fly through the air and your front end smacks into the far side. Speed bumps are often found in villages and towns, and range in height from minor to major; you can bust a wheel on the bigger ones.

Fifth, don't travel at night. As my Baja guru, Kurt Grife, likes to say, "It's hard to see a black cow lying on the black asphalt on a black night." Amen.

All gas stations are the property of PEMEX, *and the green pump with 92 octane (perhaps) Magna Sin is what you want.*

The unpaved roads are quite another matter, as they can range from very good to very, very bad. In this book I have devised my own rating system for unpaved roads: X, XX and XXX.

I have used (X) to indicate a smooth, hard-surfaced, probably gravel road that anybody on a motorcycle can (or should be able to) negotiate.

Taking an (XX) road should require a lot of forethought. Remember, there might be 100 miles of good dirt road, and then 100 feet of very bad; if you can't negotiate the last 100 feet, you're headed back 100 miles. An (XX) indicates that a competent (and just what does competent mean?) rider can get through. Sport bikes and touring bikes should think three or four times before they try an (XX), because these roads can be brutal, with soft sand and washboard. They are best suited for big dual-purpose bikes, or bare ("standard" is the popular word these days) bikes which don't have a lot of plastic bits to rattle off.

If you want to go high-bucks in the hotel scene, stay at the Hotel Westin Regina near Cabo San Lucas.

Just on the northern edge of Ensenada is the new Coral Hotel & Marina, handy for those who arrive on a yacht with the motorcycle lashed to the mast.

An (XXX) road would be very tough indeed, probably limited to lightweight dual-purpose bikes. I avoid (XXX) roads unless I am on a very capable off/on-road bike.

Friend Kurt has experience with me on a Triple-X. We were going from Mulege on the Sea of Cortez along the Raymundo Road to San Juanico on the Pacific Ocean. He had a useful 350cc dual-purpose while I was laboring with an 1100cc dual-purpose machine. Since I fell down on a regular basis, and it was a heavy bike to pick up, he repeatedly had to come back and find me. Next time I try such a stunt, he has announced, he will abandon me to my fate.

The moral of the story is: Don't underestimate Baja dirt roads. And be mindful that after a hard storm, what was a good road a day ago can become virtually impassable. Pavement is pavement, unless a storm washes it out completely, but dirt is always changing.

Hotels.   By no stretch of anyone's imagination do I attempt to rate all the hotels in Baja. And my rating system may not match somebody else's idea of what is acceptable. My hotels are merely suggestions, and I would recommend you look around at others as well.

One criterion for my choice of hotels in the cities is a safe place to leave the bike at night. Out in the small towns this is not nearly as much of an issue.

Always ask to see the room; if your Spanish is weak, just point at your eye and then in the direction of the rooms. The clerk will get the idea. If it is a questionable establishment, flush the toilet and check the hot water supply.

I give vague cost ratings for the hotels I am familiar with, using $, $$, or $$$. The single $ means cheap, anywhere from $7 to $25, with minimalist furnishings; these will suit the financially handicapped, or those who genuinely like such places (I personally like the Hotel Yeneka in La Paz, and the Dunas Motel in Guerrero Negro, both very basic).

A $$ hotel is moderately priced, from $25 to $75; this is the broadest category of hotels, generally geared to a *norteamericano* view of cleanliness and comfort, though not always. Consider a foray into $$ to be slightly daring.

Beyond that is $$$, from $75 on up, and includes the big resorts in the tourist zones.

Hotels in tourist zones often have weekday and weekend rates, and high, middle, and low season rates, plus the fancier hotels add a tax of 15 to 20 percent on top of that. In Cabo, a room that costs $40 in September might be $120 in January. In Rosarito Beach, 50 miles from San Diego, a Tuesday in November will be vastly less expensive than a Saturday night in June. My rating is based on what I think the average cost for one person would be.

I have included phone numbers with the hotels, usually the local number, preceded by that town's area code. Many of the big tourist hotels have U.S. phone numbers for ease of contact, for those who like to be reassured that a bed awaits them. I travel without reservations and have never had to spend the night in a ditch. I also recommend negotiating a deal on the spot, as a pre-booked room is going to have a set price, while a manager or owner might be willing to wheel and deal a bit to fill an empty bed.

Baja California (Norte)

Cityscape Tijuana

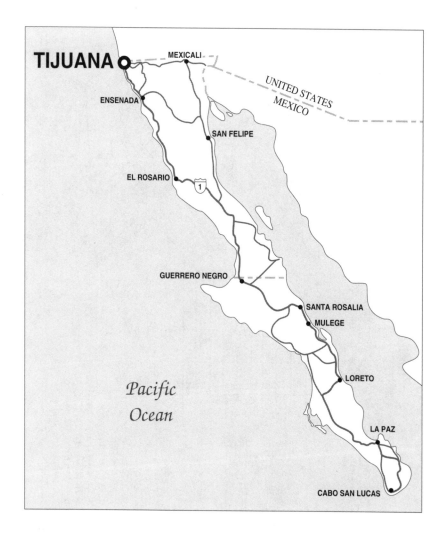

TIJUANA

MEXICALI

ENSENADA

UNITED STATES
MEXICO

SAN FELIPE

EL ROSARIO

1

GUERRERO NEGRO

SANTA ROSALIA

MULEGE

Pacific Ocean

LORETO

LA PAZ

CABO SAN LUCAS

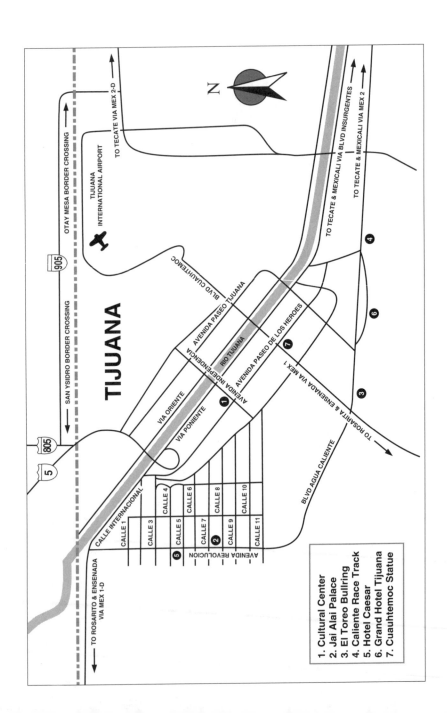

4 Sin City Redux

I hate to start off this book with a trip to a place I don't like much: Tijuana. But you've got to do what you've got to do.

When I cross the border at San Ysidro, I'm only interested in getting beyond Tijuana. It is noisy, dirty, crowded, and no fit place for any self-respecting motorcyclist. It is easy to get lost, and the traffic is always brutal. However, since some 15 million tourists visit the place every year, I should at least give it a quick once-over.

TJ was a tiny place until well into the 20th century, but it's been around for quite a while. Looking in my 1881 atlas, I see the **Rio Tia Juana,** and a little bit south, a village named Tia Juana. The place was apparently settled to support local ranches in the area, but the origins of the name are lost in the mists of time. My favorite story is that there was a ranch owned by a pleasant lady named Juanita who was referred to by the locals as Auntie *(Tia).* Whatever.

The town had a small customs post, and from 1891 a sturdy bridge over the Tia Juana River. A small resort was built at **Agua Caliente,** a little east of TJ. In 1911, during one of Mexico's many revolutions, it was "liberated" by a ragtag mercenary army, and an enterprising Californian,

We are on the Tijuana side of the border, looking back to the United States: a lot of traffic passes through here.

*Just what every
drunken tourist
wants—a photo
of himself with a
zebra-painted
donkey to send
back home.*

Dick Ferris, came up with a novel notion of how the army (less than a hundred men) could support itself. San Diegans were invited to come down and pay a dollar for the privilege of "looting" the place; there was probably not much to pillage, since the population at the time numbered less than 700. Ferris then proposed declaring Baja California an independent republic, with Tijuana as the capital. That didn't fly, either.

With the American ratification of the **Volsted Act** (Prohibition) in 1919, a new entrepreneurial spirit began stirring in Tijuana. "*¡Caramba!* If those silly *gringos* are going to do away with alcohol, we can sell it to them here. And while we're at it, we could include a little gambling. Maybe some ladies of easy virtue . . ."

And before you could say *la cucaracha,* TJ was developing a rep as **Sin City.** Deserved, too, I might add. San Diego had a lot of servicemen who needed comforting.

Sin was a major attraction up through the 1950s, but with the attention placed on family values in the early 1960s, the atmosphere changed a little. Ride down **Avenida Revolucion** in the center of the old town, and the place is a bountiful tripper-trap—all seemingly on the up and up, with the most obvious sin being the excessive intake of alcohol. You'll discover lots of zebra-striped donkeys with which to have your photo taken, charming Indian ladies sitting on the pavement selling trinkets, and San Diego college kids barfing off the upstairs terraces.

On the corner of Ave. Revolucion and Calle 8 (can't miss it) you'll find **El Fronton Palacio de Jai Alai** (The Jai Alai Palace). Jai Alai is an exceedingly fast game, rather like handball but at twice the speed, and it is a betting sport in Mexico. Games are played Friday through Wednesday, beginning about 8 p.m.; entrance is $2 to $5, and the parimutuel system is in full play.

If you want a taste of the way things were, park the bike in the guarded lot at the Jai Alai Palace and stroll down the avenue to the **Hotel Caesar** ($$; phone (66) 85-1666) on the corner of Revolucion and 5th. The long, dark wooden bar was where the gentleman of influence spent the hot hours of the day back in the 1950s. It's still a nice place for a meal—claims to be where the Caesar salad originated.

Stroll back up the other side of the avenue, and just before you come to 7th, go down the stairs into the **Unicorn Club.** Nope, the vice squad hasn't been through there in a while. This place, a holdover, one of many in Tijuana from the days of good, old-fashioned sin, is not for those concerned about family values.

Anyway, the gentlemen of influence have migrated a

Mariachi bands are for rent all over Tijuana.

few miles east to the **Grand Hotel Tijuana** ($$$; phone (66) 81-7000; U.S. 800-336-5454) at Blvd. Agua Caliente 4500, or the **Corona Plaza International** ($$$; phone (66) 86-2345) at Blvd. Agua Caliente 1426, convenient to the race track and the El Toreo bullring. Or maybe the **Pueblo Amigo Holiday Inn** ($$$; phone (66) 83-5030) on Ave. Paseo de los Heroes at the corner of Via Oriente.

The relatively new **Centro Cultural Tijuana** (Cultural Center), at the corner of Los Heroes and Avenida Independencia celebrates Mexican culture and serves to remind the Tijuanese that they belong to the United States of Mexico, not the United States of America. It has a museum and a stage, but its big draw is the **Omnimax movie theater** which shows an impressive film, *El Pueblo del Sol,* on the manifold glories of all Mexico. It is open daily from 11 a.m to 7 p.m.

The **El Toreo bullring,** at Blvd. Agua Caliente 100, is Tijuana's original arena, and a bit smaller than the one down by the sea. The bullfighting season takes place May through August, at four o'clock on Sundays (phone 852210 for full information). Tickets prices range from $8, for general admission, to $38 for a prime seat on the shaded side, and can be purchased via Ticketron, Five Star Tours (phone 619-232-5049), or at Ave. Revolucion 815 between Calles 4 and 5, or at the gate. The **Hipodromo de Agua Caliente** (Horse-Racecourse), also on Blvd. Agua Caliente, opened in 1929, flourished for many decades, then went into a slump in the 1980s when the Del Mar racetrack near San Diego opened up. Now it is called **Agua Caliente Racetrack,** and runs greyhound dogs instead; perhaps the name will change to Kynadedrome. Racing is nightly, with matinees on Saturday and Sunday (phone U.S. 619-231-1910). Admission is free.

Should you wish to seek them out, the **Tijuana Tourism Office** (Camera Nacional de Comercio, Servicios y Turismo de Tijuana), at Ave. Revolucion and Calle 1 (phone 88-0555), will be happy to burden you with lots and lots of information about the city.

Though the tourist would hardly have cause to notice it, Tijuana is still a rough city, even if the big boys wear Ar-

If you want a glimpse of Tijuana's depraved past, spend an hour in the Unicorn Club.

mani suits. Major criminals in the form of drug cartels have arrived, as this is a conduit to the United States. The local cops and the feds have been known to have shoot-outs, but this doesn't really affect us. Such things happen very infrequently, and the shooters do try to avoid hitting tourists—it's bad for the family image the city is trying to present.

However, insofar as visiting TJ is concerned, I'd recommend leaving the bike in the U.S. and walking over the bridge. If you have business with the men of influence, fine; take a limo. But if you are more concerned with seeing Baja, give the place a miss.

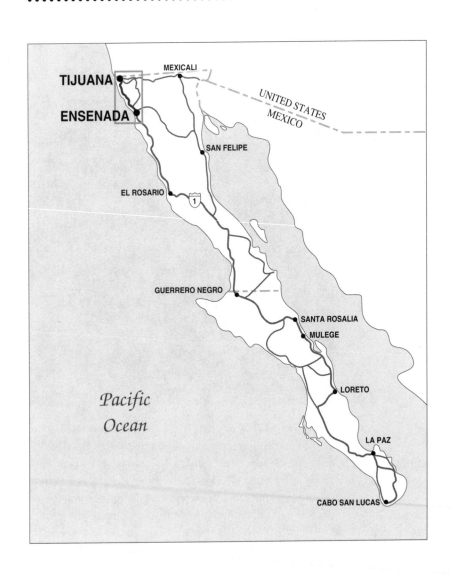

5 Roads Most Traveled

I would imagine that 90 percent of you will opt for the **Tijuana** entry. It is quick, simple, efficient—and some 15 million American tourists use it every year. Half the 200 countries on this planet have populations smaller than that.

So let us get on the road. For many of you, this may be the first time you have left the United States of America, but nothing dramatic happens.

You are cruising down I-5 into **San Ysidro,** California, ten lanes wide, border coming up, last turn-around sign goes by, and there in front of you are a dozen toll booths. There's nobody in the booths, but brown-uniformed border officials stand just to the far side, waving you on. Trucks stay over to the right, you move to the left.

About the only import the Mexicans frown upon is guns, although if you are going to Baja to hunt you can get a firearm permit from a Mexican consulate. On the return to the U.S., you are allowed $400 worth of goods duty-free, including one liter of booze. It is inadvisable to import illegal drugs. Since bikes cannot carry that much, the U.S. Customs officials will usually just look at you with half an eye, and wave you on. You're in Mexico! Hurrah!

Now what?

If you want to get your tourist card stamped here (Chapter 2, Paperwork), pull over to the right and ask for **Migracion.** You will be directed to the second building.

There will be lots of people about, from insurance touts (Chapter 2) to taxi drivers, to police and officials. They're all very pleasant, understanding that tourism is the main business of this city of well over a million people.

Puerta Mexico (an arch) reaches over the road not a hundred yards from the toll booths. **The Tourist Information Office** is on the right, should you wish to clutter up your tankbag with a few hundred brochures.

The Toll Road from TJ to Ensenada

• •

Distance   *65 miles along Mex 1-D (toll road)*

Terrain   *Roll through a few hills between the border crossing and the sea, then bolt down the coast for 60 miles.*

Highlights   *This is a quick way out of Tijuana, with few trucks to compete with. Stop at El Mirador lookout at Punta Salsipuedes.*

Mile 0   Head away from the border. Big signs overhead show the way to the TOURIST CENTER, ENSENADA CUOTA, and RIO TIJUANA. Pay attention; stick to the middle route to **Ensenada Cuota** (*cuota* means cost, as in toll road), which will make a complete circle, passing under itself, to take you along Avenida Internacional which parallels the frontier.

This is the easiest way out of TJ. Ensenada Cuota, also referred to as ENSENADA SCENIC ROAD on many signs, was built to help siphon the Ensenada-bound *gringos* right from the border to the sea and on down the coast.

Avenida Internacional is not a very pretty sight; it's rather tatty, in point of fact. A ragged fence with lots of holes in it is to your right, forming a very unprepossessing international boundary. The road is four lanes wide, with traffic pulling in from, and going off to the left. The road continues straight, starting to climb steeply, until you get views over the boundary fence to the U.S., a large estuarial expanse with an occasional green U.S. Border Patrol vehicle roaming about in the distance.

Mile 3   As the road crests the hill it turns to the left and descends, becoming the northwest end of **Libramiento,** the half-circular loop road that circles around the south of Tijuana.

> If you continue on the Libramiento loop road, you will come to the Old Ensenada Road, Mex 1, after 6 miles, and to the Tecate Road, Mex 2, after 4 miles.

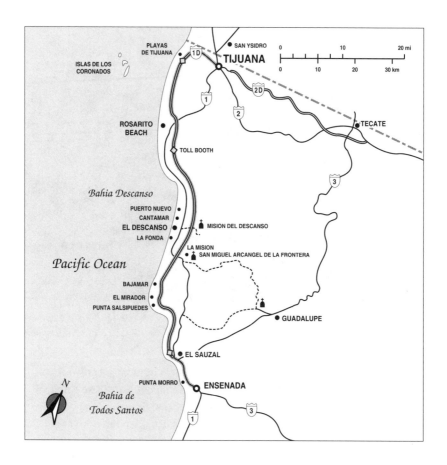

Mile 3+   Take the first exit to the right, well-marked as ENSENADA CUOTA.

Staying on Mex 1-D, the four-lane road goes up and over the **Cerro de Piedras Grandes,** and then the **Pacific Ocean** is in view.

Mile 5   This is the well-marked exit to **Playas de Tijuana,** a beach-side suburb. Its main attraction is the **Plaza de Toros Monumental,** or the Bullring-by-the-Sea; it is larger than the one in Tijuana proper. Bullfights are held every Sunday from May to September, starting at four o'clock. Tickets run from $8 for general admission to $38 for the best seats, in the shade, and can be bought at the bullring or via Five Star Tours (phone 619-232-5049) and Ticketron—yes, Yankee efficiency has come to such spectator sports.

Forget all those silly warnings about getting sick; the fruit salad is too good to pass up, and I've never been troubled.

Playas de Tijuana has a couple of motels, but since **Rosarito Beach** is less than 15 miles away, there's no real point to staying here. You may find this spot designated "Rosarito" on the map, but it is usually referred to as Rosarito Beach; I prefer the "Beach" appendix to distinguish it from the village of Rosarito 360 miles further south on Mex 1.

A trip to the beach just to the north side of the bullring is an entertainment, as **the fence** ostensibly dividing the two nations is virtually non-existent. It is a ten-foot-tall, very rusty stretch of metal—with lots of opportunity for getting to the other side.

Mile 5+ First **toll booth**, and you will be freed of 12 *pesos*, or $1.55, either currency equally acceptable. (Two more booths await you farther down the road, all asking for the same amount.) Rest rooms and a small tourist office are available there. To save the expense of staffing lots of toll booths, the 55 miles of Mex 1-D between Playas de Tijuana and Ensenada have about 15 exits, but collect tolls only at the beginning, in the middle, and at the end.

Olé!

Bullfighting is the Mexican equivalent of our heavyweight boxing. I make no judgement as to the ethics and morality of this sport, and have seen a dozen such events in Mexico and Spain. A bullfight well done is a drama, and can be an impressive occasion; it is up to the *matadors, toreadors,* and *picadors* to provide a graceful complement to the actions of one thoroughly angry bull. A bullfight usually has six separate *corridas,* involving six bulls and three *matadors,* each matador dispatching two bulls. Granted, it is not a fair fight—the bull's chances of getting out alive are very slim indeed, as he has to dispatch all three *matadors*—but there can, and should, be grace in this execution. I really can't recommend the Tijuana fights too much, as they are put on with second-rate *matadors* and third-rate bulls. The major bullfight season is in the fall, with a minor season in the spring. ■

The most popular bullring in Baja is the Bullring-by-the-Sea.

Mex 1-D, with two lanes in either direction, is reasonably lightly trafficked, as most locals, and especially truckers, don't want to spend the money. But, beware of occasional stray dogs, bicyclists, pedestrians, and unexpected construction sites.

You've paid the fee and are hurtling southward, past a humongous number of seaside developments. The whole coast from Playas de Tijuana to Bajamar is being built up at a frantic rate, mostly for *gringo* consumption.

You will see the **Islas de los Coronados,** a small uninhabited group of islands about seven miles off shore.

Pass the **Real del Mar** exit, the **San Antonio del Mar** exit, the **Oasis Resort** exit. As the road curves inland a bit, you'll see great industrial smoke stacks and a power generating station.

Mile 17   **Rosarito Beach North,** where Mex 1 Libre (*libre* means free) crosses Mex 1-D.

Mile 21   Rosarito Beach **toll booth.**

Mile 32   **Cantamar** exit; go north one mile on Mex 1 if you are looking for Puerto Nuevo/Lobster Village, a popular tourist stop; more on this in the Mex 1 Libre section which follows.

Mile 39   **La Mision** exit, which leads to the best part of Mex 1 Libre, which you'll read about on the Mex 1 Libre mileage log.

Mile 46   **Bajamar** exit, with hotels, golf, shops, and all the stuff of a major resort. South of here the coast is a bit gnarly for developing, one reason why this bit of road was put in less than 20 years ago, and sometimes washes away in a storm.

Mile 50   **El Mirador,** a scenic stop overlooking the ocean at **Punta Salsipuedes,** with restaurant, shops, and the always essential bathrooms.

Mile 60   Ensenada **toll booth.** You've just spent less than five bucks for the privilege of avoiding local traffic.

If you are not hell-bent on getting to **Ensenada** as quickly as possible, the older, narrower (and free) Mex 1 is more interesting, if more heavily trafficked. If you are taking your time, soaking up life, it is a good alternative.

I sometimes start on Mex 1-D, go down to the La Mision exit, and then pick up Mex 1.

Life is good in Baja, and the tacos are great.

The Free Road from TJ to Ensenada

. . . .

Distance   *63 miles*

Terrain   *Climb the long hill on the south side of Tijuana following the plain surrounding Rosarito Beach, head down the coast for a few miles, then run up the canyon of Rio San Miguel, which climbs up onto and crosses the mesa, before heading back down to the coast.*

Highlights *You'll have a chance to see the new part of Tijuana, buy blankets and pottery from the roadside vendors south of Rosarito Beach, and visit the ruins of the mission at San Miguel. And the ride up over the mesa is a good one!*

Mile 0   Leave the border station, and stay to the right as the road spills off the overpass over the **Rio Tijuana** (generally dry). This will run you into **Avenida Paseo de los Heroes,** a broad avenue with tall trees on a grassy median strip, which heads into the newer, more elegant part of town. You will pass through a big traffic circle *(glorieta)* with a soaring bit of modernistic sculpture in the middle.

Mile 1+   At the next traffic circle, with a statue of the Indian chief **Cuauhtemoc** in the middle, turn right onto Avenida Cuauhtemoc and follow your front wheel. There will be a little twisting and turning as the road goes around city blocks, but the southerly intent of the avenue is unmistakeable. In half a mile you cross Mex 2, which heads east to Tecate (see Chapter 9), and beyond this intersection you are officially on the **Old Ensenada Highway.**

Mile 7   You are coming up a hill, approaching the interchange with **Libramiento,** the circular loop road, which connects with Mex 2 to the northeast, Mex 1-D to the northwest. Stay straight.

The next seven miles are Charcoal Chicken country, with a dozen roadside stands selling *pollo al carbon;* there must be a chicken factory in the area. The road is broad, four-lane, and leads right into **Rosarito Beach,** crossing over Mex 1-D.

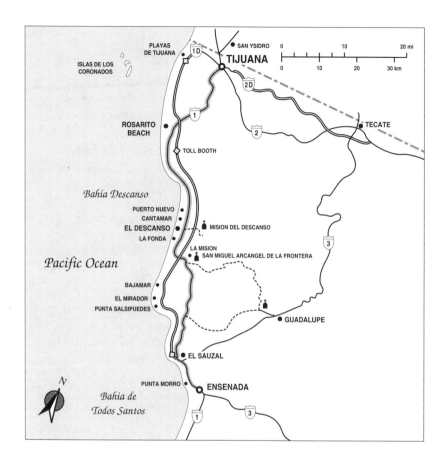

Mile 14   Taking the cruise through town on **Blvd. Benito Juarez** (old
Mex 1) is a pleasantly interesting way to view the progress of
a small Mexican city. There are shopping malls and pharma-
cies, and all the hoopla of a consumer society.

After Mexico calmed down a bit following the revolutionary period of 1910 to 1917, Rosarito Beach slowly developed a minor tourist trade, and places like the **Rosarito
Beach Hotel** (1927) and **Rene's Restaurant** (1924, and
now also a sports bar) came into being. Intrepid *gringos*
took the bumpy road (now Mex 1) 14 short miles from the
border crossing through **Agua Caliente,** over the hill, and
down to the beach. With tourism in mind, that road was
paved in 1930. Rosarito Beach is still competing with Ensenada for the *norteamerican* dollar.

California Dreamin'

The name California will now be etymologically traced. Good grief! It's a fiction! A Spanish writer, Garcia Rodriguez de Montalvo, published a minorly successful novel in 1510 called, and I translate freely, *The Adventures of Esplandian.* This knight, Esplandian, was traveling around the world and came to an island called California which was inhabited by women who were ruled by a beautiful dark-skinned queen called Calafia. And, they rode around on winged gryphons.

When the first Spaniards came to the southern tip of Baja in the 1530s, they thought the place was an island, and though it was not populated by exceptionally beautiful women, they called it California. At least that's the explanation I like best.

■

A dozen hostelries are in town, from the very basic **Marcella's Motel** ($; phone (661) 20468) at Calle del Mar 75, to the mundane **Hotel Brisas del Mar** ($$; phone (661) 22547; U.S. 800-697-5223) at Blvd. Juarez 22, on the land side of the highway. However, if you wish to soak up a little of the fast-vanishing atmosphere of the town, the **Rosarito Beach Hotel** ($$$; phone (661) 20144; U.S. 800-343-8582) on Blvd. Juarez is really the place. It has developed into a big, sprawling complex, with shops, restaurants, and a guarded parking lot.

If you do not wish the hurly-burly of the town, keep south on Mex 1, past several miles of **roadside stands** selling everything from plaster donkeys to ceramic flower pots . . . not that you'll have much room on your motorcycle for a half-size burro.

In the Tourist Zones, **bargaining** is a fully acceptable way of negotiating a price—in some places. Many of the "better" shops now have fixed prices, take it or leave it. There are no hard and fast rules in the bargaining world, but the vendors who walk along the beach selling trinkets and jewelry are probably the most likely to drop their prices—especially late in the afternoon.

Six miles south of Rosarito Beach is . . .

Mile 17   . . . the **Calafia Ocean Resort** ($$; phone (661) 21518; U.S. 800-CALAFIA), all by itself on the coast. Its claim to minor fame is that it sits on the line that divided Baja and Alta California back in 1773 and has some historical artifacts scattered about the premises, as well as an exceptionally ugly mock-up of a Spanish galleon down on the lower promenade right by the sea.

Mile 24   At **Cantamar** is the gourmand's delight, **Puerto Nuevo** (Newport, for the linguistically impaired), with more than two dozen restaurants offering their culinary delights, all of which are much the same. Lobster dominates every menu. Hotels are available for those who dissipate too much.

For those interested in Baja history, the **Mision del Descanso** (meaning "a place to rest") is just south of Cantamar. Go south one mile on Mex 1, and follow the dirt road which crosses under Mex 1-D and goes up along the stream bed to the mission. Nothing of the old mission remains, but locals have built a new chapel on the old site. Apparently the *padres* liked the area because the well-watered land in the **Descanso Valley** was good for viticulture—and wine was important to the sacraments.

Mile 27   The **Half-Way House,** selling food and spirits to Ensenada-bound travelers since 1922, still turns out a fine meal. There is nothing really noteworthy here, except the place has been around for three score and ten, and the "Halfway" moniker does put it on a lot of maps. **Art collectors** can go next door

---

A Tip . . .

The matter of tipping is bound to rear its ugly head eventually, so here goes . . . Many of the tourist restaurants include a 10 to 15% service charge in the bill. If so, I generally don't leave a tip, unless the service has been truly excellent. If the service charge is not included, I do the 10 to 15, depending on the waiter's attitude. In the little cafes along the road, where the food is very inexpensive, I like to leave a little extra just to make sure they treat the next motorcyclist that comes along with courtesy and respect.

The universal sign of the Baja tire-repair shop (llantera) is the well-placed tire; this one is especially prominent.

to the **gallery and studios** of two of Baja's better-known artists, Alfredo Ruiz and Lourdes Campos; if you do choose to buy, shipping can be arranged.

Mile 38   Mex 1-D spills off here, right between **Hotel La Mision** ($$; phone U.S. 310-420-8500) and the seriously funky **Hotel La Fonda** ($$; no phone, and proud of it). Good spot, the latter,—sort of a redundant name, as *fonda* means inn—but a nice place, with great food, great ambiance, and 27 rooms right on the cliffs over the sea. You can tuck the bikes in close to the place and not have a worry as you stuff yourself with lobster crepes and retire to your room.

Mile 39   Mex 1 goes under Mex 1-D and inland to the village of **La Mision.** The stretch farther down the coast was considered unroadable (i.e. could not build a road through there) until 30 years ago. This old road went up along the **Rio San Miguel,** crossed the river, and then climbed the bluffs to the mesa.

Mile 40   Right after the river crossing, on a long bridge, the road turns to the left, On the left is a school, and on the school grounds are the remains of the mission of **San Miguel Arcangel de la Frontera,** the adobe protected by a roof from the rain. The kids will love it if you stop, because the arrival of a motorcycle or two is always an excuse to disrupt a class. However, there is not much left of the mission to see.

On an historical note, the Dominicans and Franciscans built their Baja missions the easy way, out of adobe bricks, and these have not fared well over the past 200 years. On the other hand, the Jesuits, who had a long-term approach to religion, built their missions out of stone, and many are in excellent condition today.

The road climbs up on a mesa, passing several remnants of the long-vanished tourist trade. About the only traffic is the occasional truck avoiding tolls, and a few sightseers.

Mile 51   A dirt road (XX) goes off to the east to connect with **Guadalupe** on Mex 3 some 15 miles away.

The road starts a winding descent—be cautious.

Mile 58   Mex 1 comes out to the coast at **El Sauzal** just half a mile south of the last toll booths for 1-D. The coastal road is four lanes wide with a median strip. El Sauzal is an industrial and fishing town, of interest to the businessman but not the tourist. A man-made port houses a small number of fishing boats.

A little farther along is **Punto Morro,** and then the **Autonomous University of Baja California,** with big buildings on the sea-side of the road.

Mile 63 The highway splits, with SAN QUINTIN and ENSENADA ORI-ENTE to the left, ENSENADA CENTRO to the right.

Right by the intersection is a turn-off to the **Coral Hotel & Marina** ($$$; phone (617) 50000; U.S. 800-94-MARINA or 619-523-0064)—nice place, for $150 a night in a standard suite. If you want to go high-zoot, the Presidential Suite will set you back $660. The hotel was opened in 1995, and was well done. You'll find good art on the walls, an extensive menu, and an artificial marina. If you do stay here, you are still several miles from the heart of the city.

Stay to the right at the intersection, and head down to the port of **Ensenada** and the center of town.

Take the old Mexico 1 north from Ensenada, rather than the toll road, for a beautiful untrafficked ride where you can see the remnants of the disused tourist facilities crumbling away.

Cityscape Ensenada

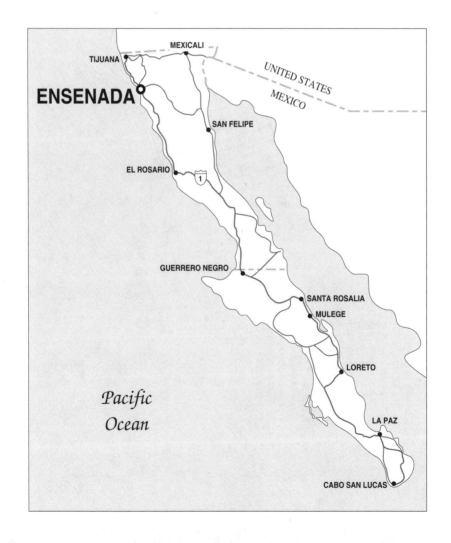

MEXICALI

TIJUANA

ENSENADA

UNITED STATES

MEXICO

SAN FELIPE

EL ROSARIO

1

GUERRERO NEGRO

SANTA ROSALIA

MULEGE

LORETO

Pacific Ocean

LA PAZ

CABO SAN LUCAS

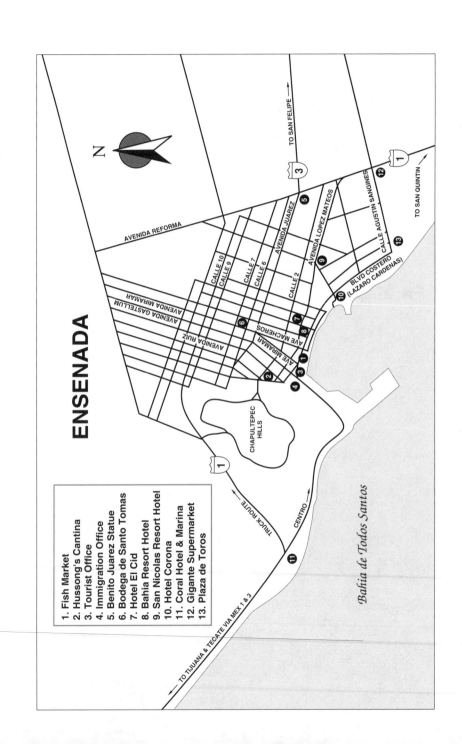

ENSENADA

N

1. Fish Market
2. Hussong's Cantina
3. Tourist Office
4. Immigration Office
5. Benito Juarez Statue
6. Bodega de Santo Tomas
7. Hotel El Cid
8. Bahia Resort Hotel
9. San Nicolas Resort Hotel
10. Hotel Corona
11. Coral Hotel & Marina
12. Gigante Supermarket
13. Plaza de Toros

CHAPULTEPEC HILLS

AVENIDA REFORMA

AVENIDA GASTELLUM

AVENIDA MIRAMAR

AVENIDA RUIZ

AVE MIRAMAR

AVE MACHEROS

CALLE 10
CALLE 9
CALLE 7
CALLE 6
CALLE 2

AVENIDA JUAREZ

AVENIDA LOPEZ MATEOS

CALLE AGUSTIN SANGINES

BLVD COSTERO
(LAZARO CARDENAS)

TO SAN FELIPE →

TO SAN QUINTIN →

TRUCK ROUTE

CENTRO

← TO TIJUANA & TECATE VIA MEX 1 & 3

Bahia de Todos Santos

6 The City By The Bay

Few natural mooring spots exist along the California coast, so when the Spanish explorer Juan Cabrillo sailed his square-rigger into this gorgeous bay in 1542, he gave thanks to Saint Matthew by naming the place in his honor.

Sixty years later, in 1602, another intrepid adventurer, Sebastian Vizcaino, anchored there. He decided to expand the role of the honored by changing the name to "Ensenada de Todos Santos" (Bay of All Saints). The fishing village that grew up there become known simply as **Ensenada** (The Bay); I suppose people have since been too busy earning a living to do any more renaming. Now this secluded body of water is often referred to as Ensenada Bay, a bilingual redundancy if ever there was one.

The tourist markets of Ensenada sell strange souvenirs; stranger still is that Americans buy them.

Nothing much happened in Ensenada until 1870, when gold was discovered in the area. Not surprisingly, life perked up. Then, in 1882, Ensenada became the capital of northern Baja California and acquired a small importance as a bureaucratic stronghold.

A few years later, in 1892, a publican named J. D. Hussong set up his cantina, and his descendants have prospered ever since. The Hussong family owns a good deal of prime real estate, and the name is seen frequently in Ensenada. I would not be surprised to see Hussong's Cantina franchises in Alta California before long.

In the early 1930s, *norteamericanos* came here to drink and gamble, but the U.S. repeal of Prohibition in 1933, and the Mexican outlawing of gambling in 1935 knocked the bottom out of that particular market.

Now it is a major port and tourist center, and home to some 200,000 residents. Tourists love it; they can get on a cruise ship in San Diego, sail down the coast, spend a day strolling the trinket markets along **Avenida Lopez Mateos,** and get back on board to sleep in clean *gringo* sheets—a pretty dull way to travel, in my mind.

As the Mileage Log for Tijuana to Ensenada shows (Chapter 5) , you enter the city by coming down Mex 1. Where Mex 1 splits, the trucks go left, circling behind **Colinas Chapultepec** (Chapultepec Hills) and rolling through east Ensenada along Calle 9 and Avenida Reforma. It's

A Word About the Word

Gringo is a Spanish word from Latin America which used to denote somebody who had blonde hair, but its meaning has since become broadened to mean anybody who comes from the U.S. or Canada. It used to be mildly pejorative, but now has come into common parlance and is used by *gringos* and Latinos alike to indicate *norteamericanos.* One of Mexico's leading authors, Carlos Fuentes, wrote an excellent novel called *The Old Gringo,* which was critically acclaimed on both sides of the border and made into a very good movie. ■

This boat, once used to ferry people from Los Angeles to Catalina Island, was sold to some people who wanted to turn it into a floating casino in the Bay of Ensenada. It's been sitting at the end of this jetty for the last ten years, waiting for that elusive approval.

about as romantic as trying to get through Chicago on U.S. 20.

Take the right marked CENTRO. As the road runs along the coast you'll see the tops of ships in front of you. When it turns sharply 90 degrees to the left, you'll be traveling parallel to the wall along the port.

Inside the port are a fishing fleet, berths for cargo vessels, a boat-building yard, and terminal space for cruise ships. The gatekeepers will probably tell you you can't come in with your motorcycle—although I have convinced them on occasion of the harmlessness of my visit.

Much of the Ensenada economy is dependent on these **cruise ships,** which sail down from San Diego or Los Angeles and debouche hundreds of shopping-mad tourists to run wild in the streets. After taking a taxi back to the ship, they nurse headaches on the trip back north.

Go along the divided highway that runs along the wall, with *topes* (speed bumps) every couple of hundred feet.

Just as the wall ends, you will see a Mexican flag on the left (three broad vertical stripes of green, white and red) and the MIGRACIONES. Cross over, park, and get your Tourist Card stamped here if you didn't do it at the border. Remember, if you go south of Ensenada or plan to stay in Mexico more than 72 hours, a Tourist Card is legally required. I have never, ever, been asked to show mine, but I am a good boy, and I carry one, duly stamped.

Just beyond the MIGRACIONES the road forks. Bear right onto a broad, divided avenue called either **Boulevard Costero** or **Boulevard Lazaro Cardenas** (makes no matter— *costero* means coastal, Cardenas was president back in the 1930s), which passes in front of the fish market, the sportfishing terminal, and the civic plaza.

The locals are in the process of developing plazas along Cardenas to lure money out of the tourist pocket, but the real pleasure is the **fish market.** It's a seriously fishy place, with tuna, albacore and red snapper fresh off the boats. All around are *taco* joints serving fish and shrimp *tacos* and hawkers hawking every sort of souvenir imaginable.

Parallel to Cardenas, and one block inland is the main tourist alley, **Avenida Lopez Mateos** (Mateos was president in the 1960s).

My recommendation for a place to stay, suitably downtown, is the **Bahia Resort Hotel** ($$; phone (617) 82103; fax 81455), fronting onto Ave. Lopez Mateos, with parking access and 24-hour guard. From here you can walk to wherever you wish to go.

Other choices on Ave. Lopez Mateos are the two Best Westerns, **Casa del Sol** ($$; phone (617) 81570; U.S. 800-525-1234), and **El Cid** ($$; phone (617) 82401). Half a block off Lopez Mateos on Avenida Blancarte is the **Ensenada Travelodge** ($$; phone (617) 81601; U.S. 800-255-3050). A couple of blocks south along Lopez Mateos, at the intersection with Avenida Guadlupe is the **San Nicolas Resort** ($$; phone (617) 61901). Behind that is **La Pinta** ($$; phone (617) 62601; U.S. 800-336-5454), one of a small chain of six rather boring hotels in Baja between Ensenada and Loreto.

For many people, going to Ensenada demands a trip to Hussong's Cantina, in business for more than 100 years and now making lots of money off the tourist trade. It's a dive, but a mildly interesting dive if you enjoy loud gringo drunks.

Down at Ensenada's fish market 20 or more little booths sell fish tacos, fish soup, fish whatever.

If you want to be on the waterfront (which is not terribly romantic, I must say), go south on Blvd. Cardenas to the **Hotel Corona** ($$; phone (617) 60901; U.S. 800-522-1516). It's a high-rise place with all the amenities, right on the bay, and only a15-minute walk to where the action is.

Food is all over. Upscale Ensenada folk like to breakfast, lunch, or dine at **Bronco's Steak House** at the corner of Ave Lopez Mateos and Guadalupe. Bronco's is located just outside the main tourist zone, and middle-class locals like it for the efficient way it is run, more or less on American lines; it is upscale because downscale locals cannot afford it.

Mexican food done to American taste is a specialty of **Cafe Hussong,** upstairs in the Hussong Plaza on the corner of Mateos and Ruiz, a couple of doors down from **Hussong's Cantina.** The cantina's decor is nothing to write home about: just a great big room, with a bar down one side, and tables and chairs everywhere else. It mostly attracts American citizens who come all the way to Ensenada to get stinking drunk and boisterously rowdy. There is no social or cultural redemption to this joint, but since it has acquired a certain drunken cachet amongst Baja travelers, it is suitable to drop in late in the evening—just to say you've been there. On weekend nights, it has all the qualities of a mis-managed zoo; hours begin at 10 a.m. and ostensibly end at 2 a.m.

American fast-food franchises are moving in, just in case you can't bear to be away from Pizza Hut. I don't believe the FFFs in the tourist zones have made any interesting ethnic alterations in their menus, as they are catering to an American, rather than Mexican, clientele.

For those who like the taste of the grape, the Santo Tomas winery has a tasting room, **Bodega de Santo Tomas,** about six blocks east of Mateos at Ave. Miramar 666, a continuation of Ave. Macheros. Two bucks (15 *pesos*) will get you an hour-long tour and a lot of tasting; tours are run thrice daily, at 11 a.m. and 1 and 3 p.m.

Two bike shops operate in the east end of town. **Cafelli Cycle Performance** at Avenida Reforma 231 (phone (617) 72134) is a Yamaha dealer with a few spare parts. In times of trouble, however, I prefer **Taller Baja ATV y Moto** at Avenida Gastelum 948 just east of Calle 9, a superb shop run by Alberto "Ciro" Caballero (phone (617) 8-1835). He's been in the same spot since 1960, and his storage yard proves it. Want an old Velocette? Triumph? BSA? Harley Hummer? There all piled in there helter-skelter with 500 Japanese bikes from the 1960s and 1970s. Ciro speaks excellent English and is noted by Baja enthusiasts for tweaking ATVs.

The **Ensenada Tourist Bureau** is down at Blvd. Cardenas 540 by the fish market; it is open every day, and has access to all the hotels. If you are interested in **bullfights,** Ensenada has a small **Plaza de Toros** down at the far end of Cardenas, on Blvd. Sangines; the season is limited to the summer months, and there are not many bullfights, but you can find a current schedule at the Tourist Bureau.

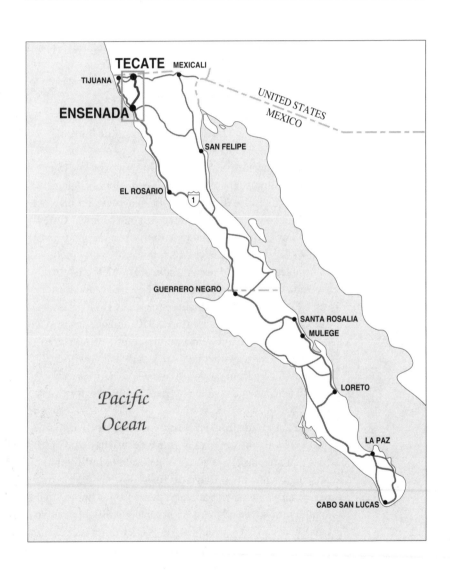

7 Backcountry Boogie

I recommend this route to anybody leaving Ensenada and heading north to return to the U.S. It's a nice ride along winding roads in open country, with several villages along the way. More importantly, the **U.S. Customs & Immigration** post at Tecate is usually not busy at all. Granted, it is open only from 6 a.m. to 10 p.m., so night riders might be miffed, but I don't think that riding at night in Baja is a very good idea anyway.

We'll begin on the north side of Ensenada, where Mex 3 angles north off of Mex 1 at a little industrial/fishing suburb called **El Sauzal.** Coming from Ensenada there is a PE-MEX on the east side of the road about a mile before Mex 3, the last for 50 miles.

The government-funded Green Angels travel all the main roads of Baja and offer free service to the broken-down tourist; how much this guy knows about fixing a Valkyrie (which was not broken, by the way) I'm not sure.

Ensenada to Tecate on Mex 3

· ·

Distance *67 miles*

Terrain *The road, lightly trafficked, heads from the coast through a small valley, climbs a bit, runs through the long Guadalupe Valley, and then climbs some more, reaching over 2100 feet, before descending along a ridge into Palm Valley. It crosses one more ridge before dropping into the small city of Tecate.*

Highlights *This is a great way to leave Mexico, as it is a nice ride on a good winding road, and the Tecate border station is never very busy.*

Mile 0 Well-marked turn to TECATE. The road wanders up a short valley, past an orphanage called the **City of Children at Rancho Coronita,** and climbs out of the valley.

Mile 6 At **Villa Juarez** a small collection of houses borders the road, and on Sunday an unmarked house (first on left) is a gastronomical goal for the Ensenadeans . . . though I've not been myself. It is a restaurant which does not seem to advertise except by word of mouth—probably to avoid the taxman.

Mile 17 Entering the village of **Guadalupe,** a paved road cuts back to the right to the old mission of Guadalupe and **Ejido El Porvenir.** The **mission** was short-lived, offering the sacraments from 1836 to 1840. The *padres* decamped to safer zones when the local Indians decided they had had enough of the intrusion.

At the intersection is a little eating place called **Loncheria la "Y,"** symbolizing the three-way turn in the road. It's merely a wooden shack with a small canopy and a single table out front, but the ladies cook well. Too many *gringos* are put off by these outdoor cooking establishments, but I find my best food at these small places—after all, that is where the locals eat. At the "Y," I recommend the *flautas,* small *tortillas* with shredded meat rolled inside and deep fried, which come four to a serving.

Mile 21 Two huge factory-like wineries flank the road, the **Pedro Domecq** (phone U.S. 619-454-7166) to the left, **Vinicola L.A. Cetto** (phone (668) 53031) to the right; both offer tours Monday through Saturday. Baja, thanks to the *padres,* grows

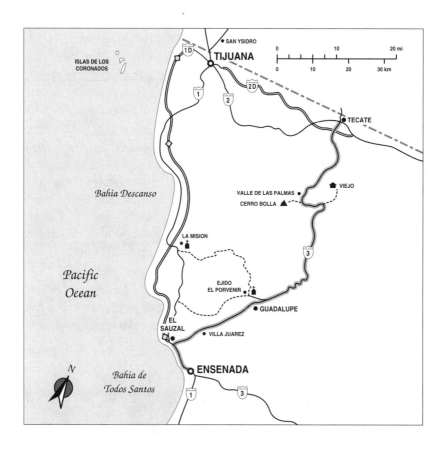

a lot of grapes, but not necessarily of very good quality. But, they are trying to upgrade the noble viticulture, and you can get some decent samplings at these places.

Try the Santo Tomas Vino Tinto. A 750cc bottle sells for 20 *pesos* ($3) or so, and it's a perfectly drinkable red table wine.

After the wineries the road rises up out of the reasonably fertile **Guadalupe Valley** into a hotter, drier clime.

Mile 48   You have gone over the high spot, 660 meters, and are winding along the ridges in a slow descent. To the right is the gate to the **Viejo** development site, an apparently doomed effort to build vacation houses in the middle of these rocky, scrubby hills.

Mile 49   The road descends into **Palm Valley.** A dirt road (XX) that goes off to the left will take you seven miles to the top of **Cerro Bolla,** a large hill some 1,100 feet high crowned with a microwave station.

Mile 50   The small village of **Valle de las Palmas** stretches out for a skinny half mile on each side of the road. A dusty PEMEX station provides sustenance for the vehicle, while the **Loncheria Las Palmas,** a/k/a **El Vaquero,** provides for the inner self. The place is clean, inclined to the northern visitor, and the English-speaking woman who single-handedly manages the place says it is open seven days a week, morning through evening. Across the road are the half-built walls of a hotel; somebody had the idea that the tourist traffic would support such an endeavor, but I think they have come to their senses.

Mile 58   On the right side of the road is a **pottery factory** and furnace, placed there because the earth is good for this work. Reddish ornamental pots and requisite frogs and lions are piled up in front. Bring a pickup if you are intent on buying.

This kiln just south of Tecate makes lots of large clay thingamajigs which are cheap here, and ten times more expensive when they get to your local import store in the U.S.

*Much of rural
Baja still
operates with
one-horsepower.*

Mile 64   An overpass! Heavens, what is that? Why, it's the toll-road, Mexico 2-D, that runs from Tecate to northeast Tijuana near the Otay Mesa (Chapter 9).

Climb up a last hill and then drop down into **Tecate,** spread out in a small valley. The road expands to four lanes, and traffic wanders all over. Off to your left on Ave. Hidalgo and Calle Caranza is the huge **Tecate brewery,** which takes up several city blocks and has its own **beer garden.** The big brewery turns out both the Tecate lager and the Carta Blanca pilsner beers. Tours are offered only on Saturdays; it is best to call to check on space availability, as they can get crowded (phone (665) 41709).

You'll bump across the rusty, weedy railroad tracks of the **Tijuana-Tecate RR,** although it is highly doubtful you will see a train.

Mile 66   At the first traffic light, signs to Mex 2 point left and right, along Avenida Hidalgo. Go up to the second traffic light, with Parque Hidalgo on your left. The cross street is Avenida Juarez, the old Mex 2 and the main thoroughfare through town. The tree-shaded park, **Parque Hidalgo,** better known simply as the **Jardin** (pronounced har-DEEN), is always very pleasant, and the **Restaurant Jardin TkT** (phonetic spelling of Tecate) located on the south side of Parque Hidalgo, two doors from the **Tecate Tourist Office,** is the place to eat. Families stroll around, and shoeshine men will bring your boots back to new if they are not too far gone—I actually had one fellow look at my 15-year-old Roadman boots and decline to do the job. I could understand why.

Several motels are along the Ave. Juarez, should you be unable to tear yourself away. Among them are the **Motel El Dorado** ($$; phone (665) 4-1084; fax 41333) at Juarez 1100, and the **Motel La Hacienda** ($$; phone (665) 41250) at Juarez 861.

Mile 67   The **U.S. border gate** is four blocks north of Parque Hidalgo. To get there, take Calle Cardenas, the street that bounds the park on the west. It's open from 6 a.m. to 10 p.m.

Folk art is disappearing in Baja; the old wood sculptor who did these statues died a few years back.

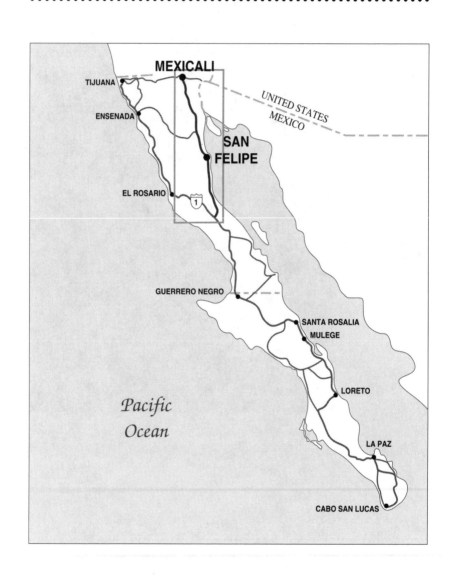

8 East Coast Approach

Those coming east from Arizona, or those headed directly to San Felipe, will probably cross the border at **Mexicali** (Mexico/California, get it?). Turn off on CA 98, which parallels the border all the way into **Calexico** (California/Mexico, the matching town on the U.S. side of the border), to meet CA 111/Imperial Avenue. Take a left and the border is about seven miles south.

If you are getting to Calexico late in the day, I recommend staying on the American side of the border at the **De Anza Hotel** ($$; phone 619-357-1112) at 233 East 4th Street. It's an old place, built in 1932, with long corridors and worn carpets. There's a guard in the parking area at the front of the hotel, and you can park the motorcycle(s) right by the door. Good restaurant.

Get up bright and early, go one block west to the main drag lined with fast-food joints and huge drug stores, and turn south. The border looms up quickly, a row of unmanned toll-like booths. Hang over on the left side, as the tourist-card functionaries are on that side. Get things stamped, if need be, and away you go.

This chapter deals with three very distinct stretches of road: the well-paved and oft-traveled 123 miles of Mex 5 from Mexicali to San Felipe, the paved and lesser-traveled 52 miles of Mex 5 from San Felipe to Puertecitos, and the 80 miles of hard dirt (XX) from Puertecitos to Lake Chapala and Mex 1.

Mexicali to San Felipe on Mex 5

· ·

Distance	*123 miles*
Terrain	*Flat, straight, and boring.*
Highlights	*Check out the funky PEMEX station and cafe at la Trinidad.*
Mile 0	Leave the border, and barrel south. **Mexicali** has about 800,000 residents and is not much of a tourist town. The souvenir shops tend to huddle up in a 20-block area on the border, just east of the entrance. It's the state capitol, a marketing center for the many agricultural concerns in the Mexicali Valley, and home to the **University of Baja California.**

Mexicali is a serious town, hot and dusty, with broad boulevards and mostly one-story houses. South of the old city, which used to be a rip-roaring place in Prohibition times, is the new city. Follow the wide avenue, Blvd. Lopez Mateos, away from the border crossing, and you'll find the **Mexicali Tourist Bureau** (phone 522376 or 525877), located at Calzada Lopez Mateos and Calle Compresora, at the first *glorieta* (traffic circle). They are open Monday through Friday from 8:30 to 2:00, and again from 3:30 to 5:00. The employees are bilingual.

Not that you'll need to go there.

Making Tracks

A little east, on the north end of Calle Calafia, is the railroad station, more or less the terminus of the Sonora-Baja RR. This line connects BC (Norte) with the rest of Mexico, but Baja itself is pretty much railroad-free. This line does/did connect with Tijuana, but had to cross the border at Calexico, travel most of the way to Tecate on the U.S. side, and then cross back into Mexico, where it is referred to as the Tijuana-Tecate RR. As the Tijuana industrial zone becomes more important, there may be other moves to resurrect a serious railway line. ■

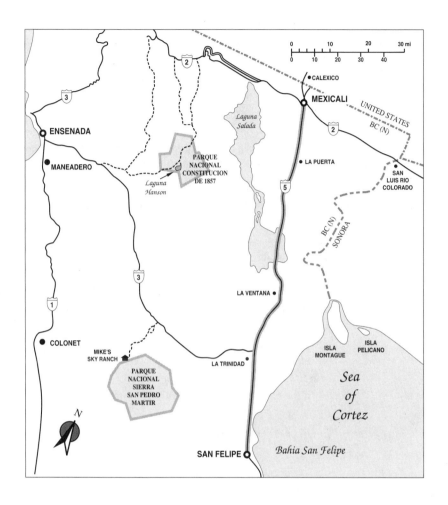

Mile 3   On the corner of Mateos at Avenida de los Heroes 201, is the new **Holiday Inn Crowne Plaza** ($$$; phone (65) 57-3600; U.S. (619) 470-3475), a high-rise hotel with all the comfort and security of home. It is within walking distance of the bullring, **Plaza de Toros Calafia,** on the corner of Calzada Independencia & Calle Calafia. The bullfighting season takes place from September through November, with two or three *corridas* a month, always on Sunday. The Mexicali Tourism Bureau will have the latest schedule information.

Stay on Calle Calafia to Calzada Lopez Mateos, thence past a second *glorieta* and on to a third.

Mile 5+   At this traffic circle, the signs for Mex 5 and San Felipe are unmistakable, with Mex 2 going left and right. Mex 5 is a straight shot south, with low mountains to the west and flat valley land to the east.

Mile 26   If you haven't gassed up in Calexico, there is a PEMEX station in the farming community of **La Puerta.** A lot of people think Mex 5 is a pretty boring road, and in truth it is, but that's no reason to let inattention get the better of you. Just to the east is the **Rio Hardy,** a small tributary of the **Rio Colorado.**

Mile 44   The road comes to **Laguna Salada** (Salt Lake), which stretches ahead for 60 miles. Back in the days of burro and shanks' mare, a lot of bones bleached out on this great white expanse of dried salt. Since the paved highway was built, death now comes to those who doze off on the straightaway. The two-lane road is elevated, and there is no room to pull off. If a truck breaks down, and night comes, it'll be sitting out there taking up half the road. In spite of this, wild and crazy Americans who need to be back in San Diego by 6 a.m. have been known to motor along at 100 mph with a load of beer in their bellies.

At the end of the lake the road rises into the **Sierra Pinta.**

Mile 71   Continue past the cafe and PEMEX at **La Ventana** (The Windy Place).

Mile 93   **La Trinidad** is an outstanding example of the failure of socialism. At the three-way intersection where Mex 3 heads west to Ensenada (Chapter 10) is a large, relatively new pink building (all closed up), which was built by the government as a 24-hour cafe and souvenir shop. There is a funky little PEMEX and cafe a half-mile south down the road which has been in business for years (and will continue so, I hope) so there was absolutely no need for this new construction. At only 30 miles from San Felipe, why bother to stop unless you just want to top off or get a soda?

Mile 122   Into **San Felipe.** This was a very, very small fishing village until 1951; a few *gringos* would fly in to try their luck with rod and reel, but that was about it. Then Mex 5 got paved, and the world changed for the San Felipians. *Gringos* drove

The outdoor restaurants on the San Felipe seafront are setting up for another day of good business.

down, trailered their boats, and wanted clean places to sleep and good places to eat. San Felipe now provides all that, with 25,000 residents, most of whom are involved with the tourist trade in one way or another.

A monstrosity of a *glorieta* welcomes you into town with two great arches that the road does not pass beneath.

Mile 123   Another *glorieta* with a PEMEX. Continue straight on down and you will bump into the seawall. **Paseo de Cortez,** a one-way street going north, has dozens of places to eat and drink; the first street inland, **Avenida Mar de Cortez,** goes south and is full of mass-produced souvenir merchandise.

San Felipe is not without its own minor charm. The town is built on the edge of a shallow bay, and the northern natural anchor, so to speak, is a modest hill 940 feet high with a small lighthouse on top. Below is a harbor of sorts, with large and small fishing boats in various stages of disrepair. The boats may be sitting solidly on sand, as the usual

The tide at the north end of the Sea of Cortez can be dramatic, leaving these boats in the harbor at San Felipe high and dry.

tides in San Felipe can run up to 20 feet, one of the curiosities of the upper **Sea of Cortez.**

Great photo op!

Many places rent dune buggies, ATVs, and dirt bikes; if it is Spring Break for Americans, the place can be zoo-like.

If you wish to be within walking distance of the action, get a room at the **Costa Azul Hotel** ($$; phone (657) 71548; fax 71549) on Avenida Cortez and Calle Ensenada. It has 140 rooms right on the beach, and the courtyard is safe for parking.

The older **El Cortez Motel,** half a mile south on Avenida Cortez ($$; phone (657) 71055 or 71056), may be a little quieter. Rooms in the new part start at $47, but I recommend an older beachfront bungalow at $57. Don't be surprised at the prices, as this is the 51st state, and the economy pretty much runs on dollars.

Food is available all over town, but my favorite restaurant is **Ruben's.** Ride out Avenida Cortez all the way to the north, and you will see the signs. It's a big rowdy place, and the fish is superb.

An alternate choice, if you don't need a full dinner, would be fish *tacos* on the Paseo Cortez.

San Felipe to Lake Chapala

- -

Distance *133 miles*

Terrain *The route begins with flat coastal land down to Puertecitos, then turns to good hard dirt (XX) and crosses over mountains that come down to the Sea of Cortez. The dirt road crosses the plain by Gonzaga Bay, twists through a short hilly stretch, and flattens out again as it crosses the dry lake called Chapala.*

Highlights *Enjoy the beautifully stark coastline south of Puertecitos, with nary a hint of green, just gray rocks, blue water, and white guano. Look forward to buying a cold drink at Coco's Corner.*

Mile 0 Gas up at the PEMEX at the *glorieta* in San Felipe and set your tripmeter back to 000; we're headed south on the **Camino del Sur** on the pavement toward Puertecitos. Past the signs for the **airport,** rounding **Punta Estrella** (Star Point), the sea vanishes, hiding just behind the sand and cactuses off to your left.

Mile 1 The turn to the **Hotel Las Misiones,** with more than 200 rooms and not a mission within a hundred miles ($$$; phone (657) 71284; U.S. 800-664-7455).

Mile 2 The turn to the newish **San Felipe Marina Resort** ($$$; phone (657) 71455; U.S. 800-777-1700).

Mile 5 The road to the right goes off to the **airport.**

Small signs indicate sandy roads that lead to several dozen beach encampments, mostly catering to Americans in trailers. Social Security goes a longish way down here.

After 30 miles the road is rather straight, begging a high speed, but signs for *vados* become common. Be cautious, and approach at a modest speed, because these wide troughs are deep enough to bottom out your forks. Hitting them at a high rate of speed is *not* advisable.

Mile 53 The road comes into the outskirts of **Puertecitos,** which has my vote for the ugliest community in Baja. There are several hundred small houses, mostly inhabited by Americans, with not a bit of greenery to be seen. The PEMEX station, cafe, and motel are sometimes operational but I wouldn't count on

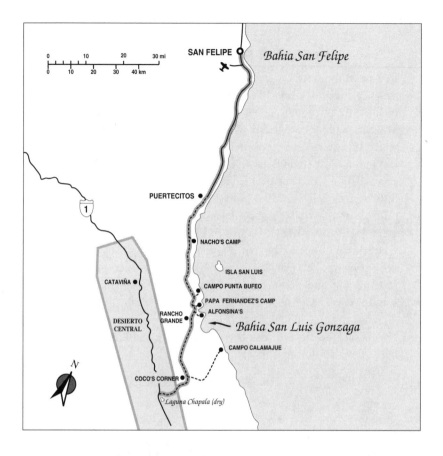

them. Commerce in town is, according to locals, pretty much controlled by a lady fondly referred to as the Black Widow.

Following your front wheel, the road continues south without benefit of pavement (XX). Several large houses have been built on treeless knolls to your left, and the road is reasonably smooth for the first couple of miles. However, you have 84 miles of dirt before you strike the pavement of Mex 1 at Lake Chapala, and most of it is washboard (see sidebar next page).

The scenery is gorgeously bleak. The road carves through shale rock hillsides, and the sea is a deep cobalt blue set off by white seagull droppings on odd rocks out in the water.

As you climb the first grade, be glad for modern road machinery. Until a few years ago, this was the first of the

Shake, Rattle and Roll

I've rated the dirt road south from Puertecitos as an (XX), which means a street bike could travel it because there are no nadgery bits, no loose rock to climb, and no loose sand. However, it does have a lot of washboard, or corrugation as it is also known—those little ripples which try to undo every bolt and screw on your bike. Washboard is a fact of dirt-road life in Baja. A 'dozer blades the road, but the tires of cars and trucks traveling over it pick up a little dirt at each turn, making little troughs between ridges. More vehicles, more little troughs and ridges. After a while it starts to look like the rippled board your great-grandmother used to wash dirty clothes.

It's not a difficult road, but it is rough, and it will shake you and your machine like a paint-mixer gone mad. Any fasteners not properly fastened will come loose. Some people try to go fast on this road, and some of those people end up stopped by the side of the road. At 15 to 20 miles an hour, all will be well.

It is said that the road will be paved one day, and I imagine it will, but I doubt it will happen in the next ten years.

Mexican road contractors spread the thinnest layer of asphalt possible, and repairing potholes is a full-time job; this stretch of road is between San Felipe and Puertecitos.

Three Ugly Sisters, three steep hills which tried the mettle of many a rider and the metal of many a machine. It was a gnarly excuse for a road. Now it is all suitably graded (if corrugated), and the Sisters go under the wheels without a whimper.

Over the edge and down at the bottom of ravines and gulleys, you'll see the rusted remnants of the cars and trucks that didn't survive the trip in the bad old days. You didn't call a wrecker back then to haul the vehicle out, you just pushed it over the side.

Mile 70   A little road with a sign leads off to the east to **Nacho's Camp,** where Americans have chosen to leave a trailer or even build a small house. Other such little housing projects can be seen along the road.

Mile 92   **Campo Punta Bufeo** is a little over a mile to the east. Here you'll find an airstrip, a row of neat cinderblock houses, and a little restaurant and motel ($15).

Mile 95   Just beyond this point is the turn and sign to **Papa Fernandez's Camp** on the northern shore of **Bahia San Luis Gonzaga,** with another airstrip, a few houses, store, cafe, and campground. Papa came down this way back in 1953, liked it, and brought his family down. Now his children and grandchildren can be found all along this northern bit of Gonzaga Bay. Papa is now pushing 100.

Mile 98   Three miles south is **Rancho Grande,** an example of what dreams and a lot of money can do. There is a reliable PEMEX, a water-purification and ice-making plant, an airstrip, a store, and the desire to build a resort to rival anything in Baja. The man behind this is Rafael Rodrigues, a wealthy vegetable grower from the San Quintin area, who wants to make this remote spot boom and bloom. Inside the store is a model of Rafael's plans, with a marina, houses, a hotel—everything a San Diego dentist could want.

If you look out to sea, a mile or so away, you will see a row of vacation homes on the beach. This is another American community, the oldest and most successful on Gonzaga Bay, with trailers and real houses cheek by jowl. It's run by the matriarchal **Alfonsina,** who, as she tells it, had a pilot friend who whacked a rough landing strip into the hardpan so he could come down to fish and lie on the beach. Gradually the word got out, and other pilots began to fly in. Not a woman to pass up an opportunity, Alfonsina decided to stay there, do a little real estate work, and open up a restaurant—and the result is rather nice. A bed in a room on the beach costs a mere $10, a shrimp dinner, $9.

Leaving Rancho Grande the road runs straight and true, and washboardy, into the **Sierra la Assemblea.**

Mile 120 Out in the middle of absolutely nowhere, where the main dirt road west to Chapala converges with a minor dirt road east to **Calamajue Bay,** you come to **Coco's Corner,** a palm-fronded, shaded area with a little shack. Do stop. Only in Baja could Coco exist. A few years ago he decided to give up the hustle and bustle of urban life in Ensenada, and came down to this bit of remoteness to set up shop, selling cold sodas and beer to passersby. You'll find my name in his guest book, along with that of just about every dirt biker who has ever come to Baja.

Coco speaks rather good English and is full of tales, some true, some exaggerated, but all entertaining. He is missing a leg, but has a solid wooden replacement. As a sideline he paints signs, like the one 22 miles back up the road indicating the turn to ALFONSINA'S RESTAURANT & MOTEL.

The road from Coco's winds through the hills, and comes out heading due west across **Lake Chapala** (dry) on a built-up berm. It's flat and straight, but very corrugated, so keep that speed down or your headlight might pop out.

Mile 133 Finally, pavement, as you meet up with Mex 1, 35 miles south of **Cataviña.**

An enterprising fellow named Coco (no shirt) has figured out how to make a living in the middle of just about nowhere, selling sodas to the few passersby on the dirt road south of Gonzaga Bay; Kurt is about to contribute to Coco's pension plan.

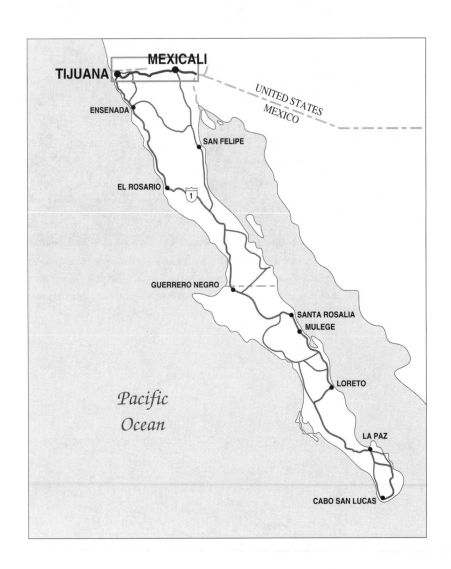

9 Along the Border

There's not much call for a tourist to use this road in its entirety, but you might well find yourself using bits and pieces of it. The **Rumorosa Grade** west of Mexicali, in particular, is a great run.

Mexico Route 2 climbing the Rumorosa Grade west of Mexicali can be an exciting ride; those who prefer less excitement can take Mex 2-D, the toll road.

Tijuana to Mexicali on Mex 2

. . . .

Distance   *123 miles*

Terrain   *The road runs from Tijuana along the spine of mountains, Sierra de Juarez on the Mexican side, Laguna Mountains on the American. It travels along the flattish high country until it reaches La Rumorosa, and then drops precipitously down to the desert floor, followed by a straight shot to Mexicali.*

Highlights   *The descent down the steep grade from La Rumorosa, called the Cantu Cuesta, is a sight to behold, and a minor thrill to ride.*

Mile 0   Leaving the **San Ysidro border crossing,** follow the RIO TIJUANA signs on the right of the multi-laner as though you are headed for ENSENADA LIBRE. Head down the divided Avenida Paseo del los Heroes to the Cuauhtemoc statue and traffic circle, staying straight to merge with Via Poniente, which turns into the divided Boulevard Insurgentes; it's a follow-your-front-wheel routine.

Alternate Route   If you truly relish being in the past, and don't mind lots of traffic, you can take the old Mex 2 through the middle of Tijuana. Turn right on Avenida Cuauhtemoc toward Ensenada on old Mex 1 and go two blocks. Then turn left at the sign indicating TECATE onto Boulevard Agua Caliente (Mex 2). **Agua Caliente** used to be a separate village many years ago but is now just part of Tijuana, and is most famous for the **bullring** and **race track** that you are now passing.

Blvd. Agua Caliente turns into Blvd. Diaz Ordaz, which runs through the busy 'burbs of **La Presa** and **La Mesa** and then out of town over the **Rodrigues Dam,** which backs up the **Rio de las Palmas** and is a major source of water for the city. After five miles, you'll merge with Boulevard Insurgentes.

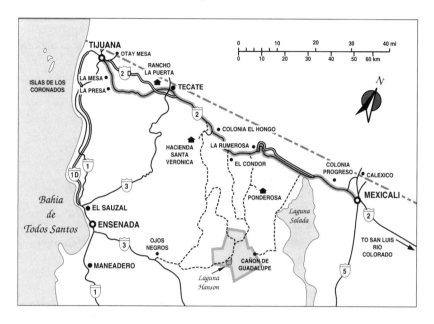

The divided Blvd. Insurgentes parallels old Mex 2, running past **La Presa** and **La Mesa,** which are the end of the suburbs and the beginning of the huge *maquiladora* industrial zones (see sidebar).

Mile 12 Insurgentes goes past the **El Florido Parque Industrial** and merges into old Mex 2. From here, the road becomes a reasonably rural two-laner, winding through the hills past an occasional little store or tire repair shop. You'll see a number of 18-wheelers ducking the tolls.

Maquiladoras 101

Maquiladoras are industrial zones established along the U.S. border. A company can ship some partially built television sets, for example, from Michigan or Korea, have a lot of the labor-intensive work done at comparatively low Mexican wages, then return them to the United States or abroad. This provides work for Mexicans and keeps the cost of a television set down. Unless we want a protected economy like the old Soviet Union, manufacturing jobs will move to where the labor costs are lowest. In North America, that means Mexico.

■

Mile 29   Access to Mex 2-D for the few miles going into **Tecate.** It's not worth the $1 expense unless your sole purpose is to hook up with Mex 3 going south to **Ensenada.**

Alternate Route   If you wish to take Mex 2-D all the way from Tijuana, use the **Otay Mesa border crossing,** the approach to which is clearly marked as you go south on I-5. Go straight south from the border for a little over a mile, turn left on the first broad boulevard (Blvd. Industrial), and head east through a heavily industrialized zone. After two miles you will come to the toll road, which will cost you $4 to get to Tecate. It is a nice road, picturesque even, and completely untraveled, running up along the **Arroyo Rio Tijuana.** Eventually Mex 2-D will go all the way to Mexicali . . . but probably not in this century.

Mile 30   **Rancho La Puerta** (phone U.S. 800-443-7566), a place that crude people often refer to as a fat farm. For a lot of money you can go and lose a little weight in very pleasant surroundings. Founded in 1940, it promotes healthy lacto-vegetarian living at healthy prices; no meat products or alcohol on the premises.

Mile 32   Coming into **Tecate,** the authorities have moved the course of Mex 2 two blocks to the south. The old route was along the town's main drag, **Avenida Juarez,** while the new route is **Avenida Hidalgo,** which runs past the Tecate brewery (Chapter 7).

Mile 34   The two avenues, Juarez and Hidalgo, meet up again on the east side of town.

Mile 36   This is as far as Mex 2-D has gotten. From here, Mex 2 climbs gently, but steadily, for 20 miles to the plateau of **El Rumorosa** at 4,300 feet, between California's **Laguna Mountains** to the north and the **Sierra de Juarez** to the south.

Mile 50   A dirt road (XX) to the right has a sign reading EJ NEJI/OJOS NEGROS 90. This is the back way past the dirt-bike hangout of

Hacienda Santa Veronica and down to Ojos Negros on Mex 3. It's an easy and attractive run if you are up for 60 miles of good dirt.

The **Hacienda Santa Veronica** ($$; phone (66) 85-9793; U.S. 800-225-2786) has become a full-on resort, with tennis courts, swimming pool, and restaurant. It used to be a bull-breeding ranch, and still offers very elementary bull-fighting lessons for interested guests.

Mile 55   **Colonia El Hongo,** where a paved road to the right connects to the dirt road to Ojos Negros. Along Mex 2 you'll notice some isolated efforts at constructing Mex 2-D, things like overpasses.

Mile 65   **El Condor,** with a PEMEX station and a dirt road (XX) to the

When it is close to Mexican Independence Day, September 16th, the vendors in Tecate's central plaza forsake the tourists and sell Mexican flags to the locals.

*Laguna Hanson
is 30 miles south
of Mex 2 in the
National Park of
the Constitution
of 1857.*

right going south to **Laguna Hanson** and the **National Park of the Constitution of 1857.**

Mile 72   Enter the elongated town of **La Rumorosa,** with a PEMEX station. A Tienda Rural Conasupo is on your right, one of a chain of cooperative grocery stores that are in most villages and small towns. Across the highway from the billiard parlor is a right turn onto a dirt road (XX) which will take you the 14 miles to Laguna Hanson and the very rustic **Rancho Ponderosa** ($; no phone).

Mile 76   Start the long descent to the desert floor, down the **Rumorosa Grade,** a/k/a **Cantu Cuesta.** The ten-mile, 4,000-foot drop to the desert floor is tough, but beautiful. The steeply descending and twisty Mex 2 has just two lanes, with lots of trucks huffing upwards or going gently downwards. On the left you will see a no-entry sign; that is the western terminus of a one-way (going west) toll road, another bit of Mex 2-D.

If you're descending the Cantu Cuesta at night, two very separate rows of headlights will be coming toward you; it looks a bit mysterious if you don't understand what is going on. When BC(N) received money to build the toll road, they got only enough to build two lanes. Even though the authorities wanted the money from tolls, they had to leave a free road, so they elected to only charge people on 2-D who were going uphill ($5 for a bike—ouch). Mex 2 remains a two-way road and the two roads run side by side for about 15 miles coming across the desert.

Mile 99   You are coming across the flats of the **San Felipe Desert,** and a dirt road (XX) heads south for 35 often sandy miles to the **Cañon de Guadalupe,** ($) which has hot springs, a store, campground, and weekend crowds.

Mile 107   The **Solidarity Monument** commemorates the beginning of BC's Big Road, the westerly Mex 2-D toll road that will bring Tijuana into the Mexican mainstream. It may be a long, long while, however, before it is finished.

Mile 114   The village of **Colonia Progreso,** with a PEMEX, marks the western edge of the **Valle de Mexicali** and its agriculture.

Mile 118   A major junction with a big road going off to the left marked CENTRO/CALEXICO, is a short-cut to the border.

Mile 123   Mex 2 intersects with Mex 5 at a traffic circle.

Mex 2 continues east 40 miles to the Colorado River and crosses over into **San Luis Rio Colorado** in the Mexican state of **Sonora** (lots of Mexican towns are named after Saint Louis, Bishop of Toulouse, so each has its defining surname). Mex 2 continues on to Sonoita and mainland Mexico. Proper paperwork is required after **Sonoita** (see Chapter 2).

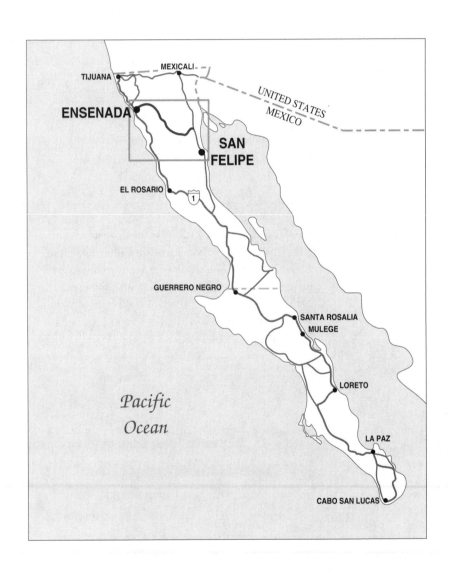

10 From Ocean to Sea

··

This stretch is a good ride—with Mex 3 rising out of the Pacific plain to cross over the low mountains before entering the high valleys of central Baja. It is the easy way to get to **Laguna Hanson** and **Mike's Sky Ranch,** and a far more interesting route to get to San Felipe than Mex 5 (Chapter 8).

This road was used in the mid-1980s for the **La Carrera** motorcycle road race, a semi-formal affair intended to be fun. The Baja authorities officially closed the road, and for a few hours it was an old-fashioned on-the-highway kind of race. There were all sorts of classes for singles, twins, and triples, but the fast four-bangers were barred. One year they ran Ensenada to San Felipe, the next year San Felipe to Ensenada. However, some riders got overly enthusiastic, several accidents occurred, and the race was abolished in 1987.

When you ride it today, imagine what it was like going flat out on your Yamaha SRX-600 or Harley-Davidson FXRS—and keep your pace to a moderate speed.

At Mike's Sky Ranch, the dirt bikes are wheeled right into the compound.

Ensenada to (near) San Felipe

. . . .

Distance   *119 miles*

Terrain   *The road is quite twisty, leaving seaside Ensenada and climbing into the Sierra de Juarez. It then passes through several high valleys, crosses over San Matias Pass and the Peninsula Divide at nearly 3000 feet, and descends to almost sea level by the time it arrives at Valle La Trinidad.*

Highlights   *Take a sidetrip to Mike's Sky Ranch, which is Baja heaven for dirt-donks and dual-sporters.*

Mile 0   Start on Mex 1 in Ensenada, having taken Avenida Reforma through the east part to the traffic light at the five-way intersection/traffic circle in front of the **statue of Benito Juarez.** Turn left onto Calzada Cortez and you are on Mex 3 headed to San Felipe. On the way up the hill there is a PEMEX station.

Mile 1   Just beyond a second PEMEX, take a well-marked left turn onto Mex 3; if you go right you will be on the **South Circular Road** heading back toward the bay.

Along the highway you will see repair shops, junk yards, and an emergency vehicle outfit (RESCATE). RESCATE gets a lot of use, but you will never have need of them since you'll be riding safely—which means you will approach each corner as though there is a big truck headed toward you straddling the middle line. In truth, my worst moments in Baja have involved tourists in motorhomes, not local drivers.

Mile 6   An amusement park, **Rancho La Paz Recreo,** is off to the left—very simple and basic by American standards, with no fancy rides, but the essential merry-go-round, dodge'em cars, putting course, and House of Fun for children.

Mile 12   Climb up past the **Piedras Gordas** (Fat Rocks), and then wind downhill briefly, before going up some more.

Mile 13   Down a short dirt road (XX) to the right is **Rancho Agua Viva,** a park where Ensenadeneos come on Sundays to have picnics and play soccer.

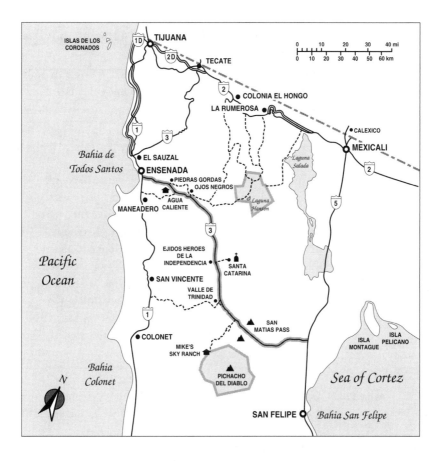

Mile 16   Just after you pass the small hand-lettered sign warning 83 CURVAS DE AQUI A OJOS NEGROS (83 curves between here and Ojos Negros), a dirt road (XX) goes steeply down to the right to **Rancho Agua Caliente** ($; no phone). If you want a pleasant ride to see a real old-fashioned Mexican resort, go five miles down the road. At the end is a sprawling complex, usually quite empty, with a sign forbidding the presence of alcohol. During holidays, the 30 rooms are packed with families, and the big swimming pool is full of warm water and people; the rest of the time you will find only a few groundskeepers—it may not be a good place to rely on for a bed and a meal. If you feel like a 20-mile hike on foot, you can follow the **Rio Agua Caliente** down to **Maneadero** on the Pacific coast.

Mile 23   You have come into the **Valle de Ojos Negros.** A PEMEX is on the right.

Mile 24   A short paved road on the left goes to the town of **Ojos Negros** (Black Eyes), a farming community in a broad, reasonably fertile valley.

Sidetrip   For a nice dirt jaunt, go to the end of the pavement in Ojos Negros, and take a right along a dirt road (XX) going straight east across the fields. After five miles, you have a choice: to the left, the dirt road (XX) goes 50 miles north to meet up with Mex 2 at **El Hongo** (Chapter 9), while straight ahead, the dirt road (XX) will take you into the **Sierra de Juarez** and lead you to **Laguna Hanson** and the **Parque Nacional Constitucion de 1857,** and from there on to **La Rumorosa** on Mex 2, some 60 miles. The Ensenada tourists take this route.

Mile 34   A sign pointing to the left indicates a shorter, slightly ruttier, 22-mile dirt road (XX) to the Parque Nacional. Laguna Hanson, named for an American rancher of the last century, has officially been renamed **Laguna Juarez** (Benito Juarez promulgated the 1857 constitution), but nobody seems to heed the newer name. Ahead, Mex 3 curves through the hills.

Mile 56   Come over a rise and the **Ejido Heroes de la Independencia** is right there.

The old-fashioned PEMEX station and store on the north side of the highway is open early morning through late evening. The old mission village of **Santa Catarina** is off to the north (left); if you are mission-hunting and wish to go into town on a dirt road (XX), you can visit the site of the old **Santa Catarina Mission.** It was begun in 1797, destroyed by Yuma Indians in 1840, and never rebuilt. You may see local pottery for sale here.

Cross the **Llano Colorado** before coming over a ridge and starting a descent.

As you climb out of Ensenada on Mex 3 and up to the Piedras Gordas (Fat Rocks), you can see the modern equivalent of folk art.

Mile 73   You're coming into **Valle de Trinidad,** population 3,000, with a badly paved, but wide road going off to the right and into town. It is the major urban site on this route, with a PEMEX, a basic mechanic shop, and several places to eat. The **Restaurant Vista Bella** on the right side of the highways has good Mexican fare but it is closed on Sundays.

Sidetrip   If you want to take the 35-mile dirt road (XX) that runs west from Valle de Trinidad to meet with Mex 1 nine miles south of **San Vicente,** take the paved bit to the end, turn right and then left, go three miles and turn right, then follow your front wheel.

Mile 84   The well-marked turn to **Mike's Sky Ranch,** dirt-bike heaven. Mike Leon himself went to the big ranch in the sky a few years ago, but his sons are running the business same as ever. The ranch has 27 rooms, a swimming pool, and a bar. It charges $40 per person for group supper, bed, and breakfast; it ain't fancy, but it's fun (phone (668) 15514).

The occasionally graded (up to 25 percent slopes) dirt road (XX) to the ranch is 22 miles long, and can be negotiated by a good rider on a Gold Wing if the weather is dry—much to the disgust of the dirt riders. The dirt-donks love

Planet Dirt

A few words about Baja dirt-bikers are in order. We street and dual-purpose riders go where other vehicles have created a known passage, whereas a dirt-donk's dream is to put a wheel where no wheel has gone before. Comfort on his machine is minimal, but he can raise his adrenaline anytime he wants by dodging cactus and rocks at a great rate of speed. Lightness is essential, so dirt riders usually have limited fuel capacity, and very little carrying capability. Because of this, they need to know more about the way to their destination than does a street-biker; running out of fuel in some remote canyon of the Sierra San Pedro Martir is a good short-cut to see Saint Peter up close and personal.

■

Going to Mike's Sky Ranch is another Baja tradition, along with getting drunk at Hussong's Cantina in Ensenada; but it can be a tough 22 miles from the pavement of Mex 3 to the ranch.

At the Restaurant Jalisco, just east of the San Matias Pass on Mex 3, the cowboys stop in for breakfast before going off to work.

to exaggerate artfully about their daring doing. I do suggest a visit if you have a suitable mount; it's a Baja tradition.

Mile 89   You are crossing the **Peninsula Divide at San Matias Pass,** at 2,950 feet. From here, rivers flow east to the Sea of Cortez and west to the Pacific. Twenty-two condor-flying miles to the south is **Picacho del Diablo,** the highest point in Baja at 10,154 feet. The downhill run should be treated with respect. High-country chapparal is changing to low-country desert.

Mile 94   **The Restaurant Jalisco** is to the left, patronized mostly by local *vaqueros* who may be carrying their horses in the backs of pickups just like *yanquis.* Good goat-meat *tacos.* Goat meat, which is usually young goat or kid, is very tasty, a tad stringy, and reminds me a bit of savory mutton.

Mile 106   You can see the sea.

Mile 119   Mex 3 ends at Mex 5; Mexicali is 90 miles to the north, San Felipe 30 miles to the south. At the intersection is the failed, closed, **Parador Turistico El Chinero.** A couple of hundred yards south is the most delightful PEMEX station in Baja, one great pile of antique junk.

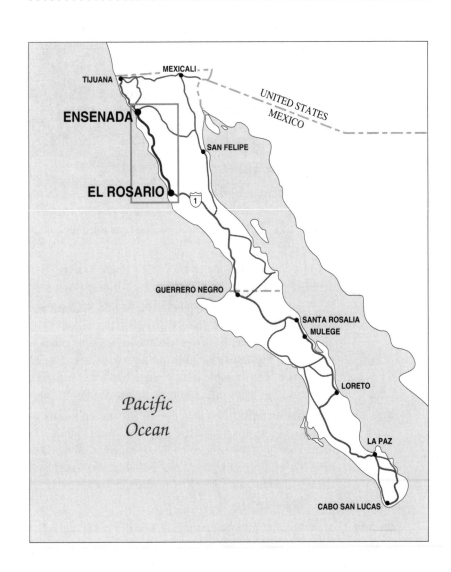

11 Where It All Begins...

Americans might not think that the earth is flat, but they do tend to believe that all reasonable signs of 20th century civilization stop a few miles south of Ensenada. I would guesstimate that of the 15 to 20 million *norteamericanos* who cross the border into Baja California every year, probably fewer than 20,000 ever go farther south than a few miles beyond Ensenada.

Ensenada is such a sprawling city, that it is hard to pick out a place to zero your tripmeter. However, since we took you to the **statue of Benito Juarez** on Avenida Reforma for the start to San Felipe (Chapter 10), we'll begin there.

If you are going along the sea-front, go half a mile beyond the bayside Hotel Corona, turn left onto Calle Augustin Sangines (90 percent of the traffic is making that turn), and up nearly a mile to meet with Mex 1 at the Gigante supermarket, where a traffic light tries to control the activity. You're just a half mile south of the Juarez statue.

Ensenada to El Rosario on Mex 1

· ·

Distance   *161 miles*

Terrain   *From the sea, the road rolls and winds through several small hills and valleys, before running flat and straight across the plains of San Quintin. Beyond the bluffs, it descends steeply to El Rosario.*

Highlights *Take a sidetrip to La Bufadora, the Baja equivalent of Old Faithful, and ride out to Punta San Jacinto to see the picturesque old freighter,* Isla del Carmen, *which ran aground years ago.*

Mile 0   Start at Avenida Reforma at the **Juarez Monument** and just head south. Whether you come through the center of Ensenada and along the waterfront, or via the Oriente (east) truck route, you will eventually end up on **Avenida Reforma,** which is Mex 1 going south.

And the city just continues on. Some suitably disreputable, graffiti-covered, apartment buildings are on the west side of the road. An occasional traffic light prevents the traffic from going pedal-to-the-metal for the dead straight nine miles to the Maneadero intersection. You'll ride past the military base and military hospital, and then by an airfield shared by civilian and military alike.

Mile 1+   A PEMEX is on the right.

Mile 5   The well-marked turn to the **Estero Beach Resort** ($$$; phone (617) 66230; fax 6925), a full-service resort, that offers jet-skiing, fishing, and lying on the sand.

The housing build-up seems to cease at the bridge over the **Rio San Carlos,** where Mex 1 goes from four lanes to two. On the east side of the road are 20 or so palm-fronded stalls dedicated to catching the returning day-tripper from La Bufadora (see sidebar overleaf), selling hot peppers in jars, olives, corn on the cob, *tamales,* strings of garlic—all that gorgeous-looking condiment.

Mile 9   **Maneadero** comes into view looking very tatty. The name, "Rein-maker," is said to derive from the fact that a harness maker lived here a long time ago; maybe, maybe not. Watch out for the *topes* (speed bumps), of which the town has about eight. They are not all marked, but the vehicle lurching

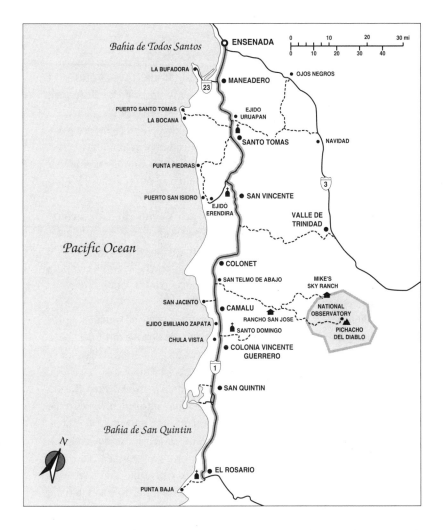

violently in front will provide you with a warning. Maneadero used to be a small junction community of a few hundred people and one PEMEX. Now it has 10,000 inhabitants, most of whom are involved in farming, and three gas stations.

Go straight (south) through the only intersection in town. The mile-long row of shops and garages is set back from the two-lane road, with roaming vehicles sending up clouds of dust from the expanse of dirt between the pavement and the stores. The old **immigration checkpoint** closed down 15 years ago. Bump over the *topes,* past the last PEMEX, and soon you will be free of commercialism.

A Trap for Trippers

At the only traffic light in Maneadero, State Route 23 goes off for 14 miles to the west, to the overly touted (in my opinion) **La Bufadora** (buffalo's snort), a tidal blowhole that is, however, worth a visit.

After six miles through flat, estuarial land, a paved right turn leads to the **Baja Beach & Tennis Club,** a failed attempt at building a resort hotel. The building was begun in the early 1980s with the notion that gambling would be legalized and this would become a casino. That has not come to pass, and the place is rather vacant.

The road goes by the **La Jolla Beach Camp** ($), an eccentric five-story structure looming over the road and several small houses, most owned by Americans. A Russian emigre began this little empire long ago, and it is now a delightfully old-fashioned place with camping on the beach. Yes, the sign does say you have to push your motorcycle, but that is only true for noisy little dirtbikes.

A short way beyond the La Jolla entrance is a (too) small sign for the **Punta Banda Cafe,** several hundred yards down a dirt road (XX). Owned by Mike, an ex-cop, the cafe serves up good food at reasonable prices: seven bucks for a large plate of garlic shrimp.

Continuing along BC 23, the road climbs up around **Pico Banda** (1,264 feet), curves around, and starts dropping into a small bay. At the top of the hill is a square water tank; turn off onto the bumpy dirt area, and 200 yards ahead is the edge of a cliff, which looks down on **La Bufadora** from above. That may be your best view of the place.

A **blowhole** is merely a hole in a rock where the tide can surge underneath and send a spout of water up through the hole and into the air. I like the legend that a baby whale swam into the underground cavern when he was very small, has grown up inside unable to leave, and the blowhole is his spouting.

Twenty years ago there was nothing out here but the blowhole. Now it has been turned into the Mexican version of Old Faithful, with a half a dozen restaurants and a carefully constructed strip of shops (complete with pay toilets) that you have to pass through. Access is free, but do not try to go there on a weekend.

The best thing about a trip to La Bufadora is having dinner at **Cecilia's Restaurant** (the fried whole sea bass is highly recommended) and then riding back over the mountain and seeing the shoreline of the **Bahia de Todos Santos** all lit up. It is a sight. ■

A Sunday afternoon at the beach, a horse, a bottle of beer—ahhh!

Several miles later, you might well find an informal **inspection station** manned by the Federal Police and the army. No worries. I've never been stopped going either way. I slow way down as I come through the orange cones and get waved on by whoever is standing at the stop sign.

These impromptu checks are prompted by Uncle Sam, who has leaned on the Mexican government to cut down on the amount of illegal drugs heading toward our border. Noble thoughts, but I doubt any smuggler with an IQ over 60 has ever fallen afoul of these cops, except during a routine shakedown of a trucker without proper papers. I look on these occasional roadblocks as a window into the fictional *bandito* past.

Mile 22   The turn-off to **Ejidio Uruapan.** A little-used dirt road (XX) runs up the **Rio Piño** and eventually connects with Mex 3 at either **Ojos Negros** or further south near **Navidad.**

Mex 1 climbs up and crosses over into **St. Tom's Valley,** with a delightfully steep descent that includes a monstrous downhill U turn. The valley once belonged to the **Santo Tomas winery,** and still produces grapes and olives, for which we can thank the *padres* of yore who had to have wine to celebrate the sacraments.

Mile 26   Turn to the left for **La Bocana** and **Puerto Santo Tomas.** This dirt road (XX), 16 miles long, follows the **Rio Santo Tomas** and ends at a small seaside fishing community.

ROAD OF SLOW SPEED *is how that sign transliterates, and the wary motorcyclist should take note.*

Mile 28   You are in the village of **Santo Tomas.** The **El Palomar** has the tourist trade sewed up, with a ten-room motel ($$; phone (617) 54011)), PEMEX, restaurant, store, and RV camp.

If you go down into the RV area on the east side of the road, go to the end and turn left through the olive grove, heading toward three very tall palm trees. You will find the remains of the mission of **Santo Tomas de Aquino,** which operated from 1791 to 1849. There is not much left, just three clumps of adobe, and nothing is being done to protect it. The El Palomar owner is missing a bet by not advertising his little bit of history and covering it with a roof.

Sidetrip   This pleasant, 44-mile excursion will take you along the coast through the last elements of Gringoland. Go 100 yards past El Palomar to the grocery store and take a right onto a wide dirt road (XX). After 200 yards, turn right again at a dirt intersection. The road then climbs up over some low hills before dropping down toward the coast. Along the stretch from **Punta Piedras** to **Punta San Isidro** there are several fishing camps and groupings of *gringo* houses.

Only the first 33 miles are dirt; when you get to **Ejido Erendira** and **Puerto San Isidro,** you are back on potholed asphalt, and will re-connect with Mex 1 after 11 miles.

Going south on Mex 1, the road climbs gently out of the Santo Tomas valley and drops into the valley of the **Rio San Isidro.**

Mile 51   The sign indicates a right turn to the ruins of the mission of **San Vicente Ferrar.** There's not much left but some adobe, but for the half-century the mission was in use, 1780 to 1833, it had a rough go. The local Yuma Indians were not happy with the papist invasion and enjoyed tormenting the *padres* and the small military contingent that protected them.

Mile 52   The village of **San Vicente** has a PEMEX, several stores, and two motels of unknown quality (I'd say, cheap).

The road again crosses a low ridge as it goes from valley to valley, this one watered by the **Rio San Antonio.** As you come over the ridge, look over your clutch lever and you will see a line of mountains to the southeast. That is the **Sierra San Pedro Martir.** On a clear day you can make out **Picacho del Diablo,** which stands over 10,000 feet high, some 45 miles away.

Mile 61   A dirt road (XX) to the left (marked LOS COCHIS 12 LA CALENTURA 14) more or less follows **Rio San Antonio** for 35 miles to **Valle de Trinidad** on Mex 3. For anybody with just a few days to spend in Baja, this makes a nice, if occasionally gnarly crossover, and you can easily get back to Ensenada or down to San Felipe.

Mile 76   Entering the town of **Colonet,** you begin a 40-mile stretch through heavily farmed land. On the right is a PEMEX which is erratically open. On the left, at the town bus terminal, is the **Restaurant Magui.** Inside it is clean, with 1950s chrome and formica, and a menu of rural Mexican gastronomical delights prepared by several cheerful women in the back. They claim the place is open from 7:30 a.m. to 8 p.m. daily.

Not much romance in this shipwreck at San Jacinto, but it makes a great photo backdrop; the small freighter Isla del Carmen *ran aground here in 1981 and was left to die.*

Room With a View

The road to the **National Observatory** is 60 miles of well-graded dirt (XX), and if you like going from seaside to high mountain, this is an excellent excursion. Keep in mind that you might be turned back at Mile 48, and that the observatory is not open to the public, but the views from the top are stunning—you can look right across the peninsula to the Sea of Cortez.

The first 17 or so miles are very good, past the village of San Telmo. The next 13 are okay, until you come to an intersection with a road to the left marked MIKE'S SKY RANCHO (Chapter 10). Bits in that 16-mile stretch to Mike's (XXX) are very steep and very gnarly, with lightweight dual-purpose bikes the way to go.

A mile farther along is the turn to the **Meling Ranch,** a/k/a **Rancho San Jose,** a dude-type ranch where reservations are essential. The mailing address is: Meling Ranch, Apartado Postal 1326, Ensenada, BCN, Mexico; or 1777 Knapp Drive, Vista CA 92084; phone 619-758-2719.

The road starts climbing up into the **Parque Nacional Sierra San Pedro Martir,** but at the gate, Mile 48, the fellow in charge will probably turn you away. No motorcycles allowed—dirt bikes send up clouds of dust which hover over the mountain top and obscure the lenses on the telescopes in the observatory. However, if there is no one on duty, or the fellow thinks your Gold Wing is a car, you are on your way.

At the 6,000-foot level you come into a heavy pine forest and the road makes a few switchbacks, going up to about 8,000 feet before running into a barrier. The observatory personnel live here and commute the rest of the way to the top on a paved surface. Tourists have to walk up this stretch. The road ends at the observatory, at 9,184 feet above the sea, only 33 linear miles away to the **Sea of Cortez** and 44 to the **Pacific Ocean.** There is informal camping near the barrier, in the **Viacitos meadows** (bring your own water). At the top of the mountain are two small peaks about a mile apart, one reaching to 10,154 feet, the other two feet lower. These were not climbed until 1911, a challenging Class 3-5 climb, in modern mountaineering lingo.

■

Mile 84   Coming into **Ejido Diaz Ordaz,** also known as **San Telmo de Abajo,** a dirt road (XX) goes off to the east, 66 miles to the observatory near the top of Picacho del Diablo (see sidebar). If you pass the **Cafe El Puente** and cross over the bridge on the **Rio San Telmo,** you've gone too far by a hundred yards .

Mile 89   From Mex 1 heading south, a large sign points the way to **San Jacinto,** a little more than three miles to the west.

Sidetrip   This three mile dirt road (XX) will take you through **Ejido Mesa de San Jacinto,** a slightly inland fishing village, and out to the coast. It's a good road, but a thin layer of drifting sand can make the handling a bit tricky and the faint of heart a bit queasy. The land curves out to **Punta San Jacinto,** where a straggling of trees is scattered about a restaurant and trailer park. Lying on its side just 150 feet off the shoreline is an old coastal freighter, the *Isla del Carmen,* which ran aground in 1981. A few *pangas* (open boats) belonging to the village fishermen are drawn up on the shore, protected by the wrecked vessel. The whole scene makes a modern romantic seascape, especially when some surfers are out catching waves in the bay.

Mile 95   The farming community of **Camalu,** with a PEMEX.

Mile 101+   You've come through **Ejido Emiliano Zapata,** then **Chula Vista.** The white and green **Baja Cafe, Restaurant & RV Stop** is on your left. At the top of the hill is a small cement bus stop with MOTEL ORTIZ advertised on top. Just beyond is a dirt road (XX) to the left that goes out to the remains of the **Mision Santo Domingo,** along the **Rio Santo Domingo;** it's a five-mile ride through rustic farming country. The mission remains are by a new chapel and school up at **Red Rock Canyon;** August 4th, Santo Domingo's Day, is a major *fiesta.*

Mile 102   **Colonia Vincente Guerrero** stretches along both sides of the road, with a PEMEX, a bank, restaurants and cafes, and all the other signs of a successful agricultural community. The small

Motel Sanchez ($) is your basic, clean, cheap Baja motel, run by, of all people, Señor Sanchez.

The highway now goes dead straight for the next 15 miles, across endless well-worked fields; when you see the well-stocked produce department in your local supermarket in the winter, the veggies might well come from here.

Mile 114 An elegant **Ministry of Tourism** office sits by itself in the fields, uninhabited.

Mile 115 The start of **San Quintin,** with a big sign advertising the HOTEL LA PINTA 20 km further on. Opposite the sign, on the left side of the road, is the **Restaurant Mision Santa Isabel,** which is run just like any such place between Texas and Southern California. Clean, efficient, uniformed waitresses, serve you from a menu in Spanish and English, though occasionally the English is slightly flawed, as in "onion liber" (liver with onions). If you stop there for breakfast, you'll run into the local farmers discussing weather and wages. Most will be eating *menudo* (tripe stew), which the locals prefer to ham and eggs. In the corner might be a couple of local big shots, with a syncophant or two hanging on. It is good-old-boy stuff with a Mexican accent, open from 7 a.m. to whenever the clients go home.

The town has a PEMEX. At the south end, just before the bridge, is the **Motel Chavez** ($; phone (616) 52005)—only $13, but clean and quite nice—with the **Restaurant Quintin** attached.

Mile 121 A big sign advertises the **Old Mill Motel & Resort** ($$; phone U.S. 619-428-2779), three miles down an occasionally sandy dirt road (XX) that goes west to **Bahia San Quintin.** If the road conditions wouldn't phase you, I would say this is a "must stop." The old mill was built in the 1890s by a British-based consortium, the Lower California Development Company. They had leased the entire San Quintin area from the Mexican goverment, thinking it was perfect for wheat; they even built a short railroad to get goods to the bay. Four years of drought, however, spoiled that idea, and they pulled up their railroad tracks and went home. The Old Mill has lovely new rooms, and an excellent restaurant with a fine bar housed in an old fish cannery that was active until the 1960s (it has been thoroughly cleaned up, I might add).

Mile 123   Another sign advertises the **Old Pier/Muelle Viejo & San Carlos Motel & Restaurant** ($; no phone), which is two miles down an occasionally sandy road (XX). It is a counterpoint to the Old Mill, a funky old place, probably built in the 1950s, with occasional water in the faucets and electricity only from darkness to about ten o'clock. I really can't recommend it, other than for nostalgic purposes. The remains of the iron posts of the old British-built pier can be seen marching out to the middle of the bay.

Mile 124   The road splits—the main route, Mex 1, angling slightly off to the left, sticking to the high ground; the secondary, which used to be the main route some years ago, goes to the right. The old road got properly washed out in 1993, leaving the crossing of **Rio Santa Maria** with close to a mile of dirt; the two roads meet again after six miles.

Mile 129   A large sign indicates the **Hotel La Pinta** ($$; phone (616) 52878; U.S. 800-336-5454) off to the left, two miles down the paved road heading to **Bahia Santa Maria.** A mile beyond the La Pinta, down a good gravel road (X) heading to **Bahia San Quintin**, is the **Cielito Lindo Motel,** ($$) with a bar, restaurant, camping, and a dozen rooms (the $30 rooms are rather large, but need a coat of paint). The first might seem tomb-like in its emptiness, the second, with a cheerful American woman running the bar, often has a pleasantly boisterous bunch of locals in the restaurant.

Now Mex 1 tears off into the undeveloped world. The sea is off to the right, and the land becomes less fertile as you go south, with scrub and rock and sand taking over. The road climbs up onto a small plateau and then starts a seriously steep, twisting descent into the valley of the **Rio del Rosario;** the sign CURVA PELIGROSA (dangerous curve) says it quite well. All sorts of strange things happen on that hill, from uphill-bound trucks stalling and blocking half the road to downhill-bound trucks losing their brakes. Not likely to happen on your watch, but a look down in the gullies can be sobering.

Back in the 1960s, Mama Espinoza aquired a deserved reputation for the lobster burritos she served at her little restaurant in El Rosario; she has long since retired, but her esablishment continues on.

Mile 160   Entering **El Rosario** (The Rosary), with a PEMEX on the left. This town has never been out of gas in my years of going through, so fill up, even if there is a line at the two pumps.

The gas station also runs a small motel ($), which tends to be noisy from passing trucks. Next to it is the well-known **Mama Espinoza's Loncheria,** famous for its lobster *tacos.* The place has been around for half a century, and Mama has long since retired, but the tradition goes on, and the prices go up.

Mile 161   Mex 1 makes a hard left, while the dirt road (XX) to the right goes out ten rough miles to a fishing and surfing spot at **Punta Baja.** This corner will be the start of the next section, El Rosario to Guerrero Negro (Chapter 12). A quarter mile up from the corner is the **Sinai Motel,** ($; phone (616) 58818), with a good restaurant, **La Marantha** attached; that is my recommendation if you are going to spend the night in this town.

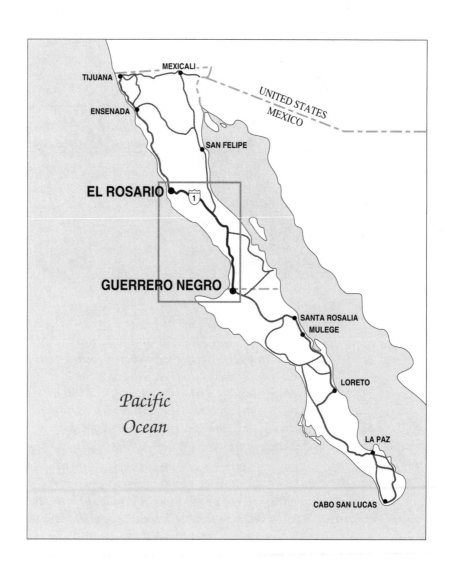

Pacific
Ocean

12 Bashing the Boojums

Fabulous riding, this bit of road, which separates the sight-seer from the true traveler. If 100,000 people go to Tijuana, and 5,000 to Ensenada, barely a hundred pass El Rosario. Perhaps I exaggerate a bit, but you get the point.

The highway south to **Guerrero Negro** generally has good asphalt, but that wasn't true until just a few years ago. In the 1960s, the road was paved as far as **El Rosario,** but beyond that were 500 miles of rough dirt. Any number of motorcyclists challenged that road on Harley panheads, BMW twins, and AJS singles, but it was not a trip for the timid.

Then, Mexico decided to complete the highway from Tijuana to the tip of the peninsula—lay asphalt, and the tourists will come. They paved, finishing the task in 1973, and lo, the tourists did not come—at least not in the droves the Mexican Tourist Commission had hoped for.

El Rosario is supplied from the north, and Guerrero Negro from the south via **Santa Rosalia** on the Sea of Cortez. In between is an entrepreneur's no-man's land, with one large hotel, one small one, two official gas stations, half a dozen unofficial ones, a few dozen places to eat, and a number of *tiendas* where you can buy anything from bottled water to canned beef.

While this stretch provides superb motorcycling, it is time again to remind you that Baja is quite intolerant of those who ride beyond their ablilities.

El Rosario to Guerrero Negro

- -

Distance   *221 miles*

Terrain   *From the coast, you ride along a narrow ridge in the Sierra San Miguel until you drop down to Lake Chapala, through the western foothills of the Sierra La Asamblea, and into the Vizcaino Desert.*

Highlights   *The landscape of the Central Desert looks like something out of a* Star Wars *movie, and the sidetrip to Mision San Borja is superb.*

Mile 0   Start in El Rosario at the 90-degree left turn by **Mama Espinoza's,** where the road goes east along the river past the Motel Sinai and Restaurant Marantha (Chapter 11).

Mile 5   The road turns south, crossing over a long bridge, and then starts to climb up on the **Pitahaya Mesa.** It is a superb motorcycle road, running along the ridges, dodging in and out, with an occasional *vado* (dip) to keep your mind alert. This is not a road to mess with; if you go off the edge, you will land on rock and cactus.

Mile 15   A dirt road (XX) goes off to the right, some 40 miles to **Punta San Carlos,** where there is a seasonal fish camp, and usually a lot of *gringo* wind-surfers.

Mile 32   The **Loncheria Descanso** (Take A Break Cafe) is at the **Rancho del Descanso,** with a great big parking area for long-haul trucks. All of these highway cafes have big, dusty pull-offs, as feeding truckers is their business. This one has good food, as well as a superb *sanitario* (toilet), with two doors and a sink outside.

Mile 38   To the right is the turn to the remains of the mission of **San Fernando Velicata,** three miles down a bumpy dirt road (XX). Those who follow the religious squabbling inside the 17th century Catholic Church may find it interesting that this is the only Franciscan-built mission on the peninsula (see sidebar overleaff).

Mile 48   A turn to the right for **Puerto Catarina,** a seasonal fishing camp some 20 miles down a dirt road (XX). The whole 150-mile stretch of coast way off to the west is criss-crossed with a network of very rough roads (XXX) that I have never

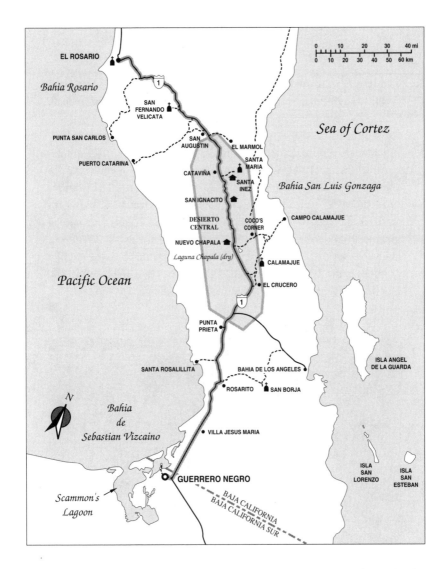

explored. Friend Kurt, who has taken his four-wheeler through parts of it, calls it the **Lost Coast;** surfers call it the **Seven Sisters,** for the seven small capes along the shore.

Mile 56   The little village of **San Augustin,** where an abandoned PEMEX station underscores the failed promise of this highway—just not enough traffic to make a go of it.

Mile 57   To the left is the turn for **El Marmol** (The Marble), an old onyx mine 14 miles down a dirt road (XX). The Southwest

A House Divided

The Jesuits were the first to bring the benefits and banes of European civilization to Baja, beginning in 1697. However, in 1767, the Spanish kicked the Jesuits out of their world, feeling that the Society of Jesus was a little too attached to spiritual matters and to the Pope in Rome. The Franciscans, under Father Junipero Serra, took their place, traipsing into this pleasant, well-watered valley in 1769, with a plan to continue their string of missions all the way to the north. The Dominicans, however, were upset at not having their own turf, and Serra realized that Baja was not nearly as promising as Alta California; he graciously conceded Baja to the Dominicans and went off to San Diego to start a new chain of missions up to San Francisco (he did like promoting the order's patron saint). It wasn't too long before the Dominicans realized they'd been had, but by then it was too late.

For the ecclesiastically curious, the mission San Fernando Velicata was founded by Padre Junipero Serra in 1769, before he moved off to proselytize Alta California.

The PEMEX *at Cataviña often has a line of vehicles, and sometimes has no gas; no worries, as gas is available at the llantera 35 miles farther south.*

Onyx & Marble Company operated from 1900 to 1958, leaving behind an onyx building (whether it was a jail or schoolhouse depends on who you talk to), a graveyard (local necessity), and some rusted mining equipment that was not worth hauling away.

Mile 60   You have now entered the **Parque Natural del Desierto Central de Baja California,** which is about 15 miles wide and 100 miles long. Do not look for a park headquarters or a museum or anything, or even a sign announcing the entrance into the park; all that costs money which the government does not have.

The park is home to a lot of vegetation that you will never see anywhere else, including the **cirio cactus,** (in botanical terms, *Idria columnaris,*) also known as the **boojum tree;** obviously the botanist who first came upon these had been reading Lewis Carroll's *The Hunting of the Snark.* This plant, which can reach 60 feet in height, is found only in this small part of the world. All along the highway, great boulders and a dozen varieties of cactus cover the horizon. To get the full effect, pitch your tent on a full-moon night.

Mile 76   The oasis of **Cataviña.** Watch out—on both sides of this place are *vados* which tend to have a trickle of water most of the year and slimy green stuff underneath. Many a motorcyclist has been surprised.

Cataviña itself has a **Hotel La Pinta** ($$; (617) 62601; U.S. 800-336-5454) on the right side of the road, with a PEMEX Green pump for the hotel clients, although sweet-talking *gringos* can usually use it. It usually doesn't work, however, between 9 a.m. and 4 p.m. when the hotel electric generator is turned off. On the other side of the road is a large, dusty PEMEX station offering both lead-free Green and leaded Blue, when it isn't out of gas.

If you can't get gas here, don't worry, you can fill up 35 miles down the road.

Next to the gas station is an abandoned cafeteria, which was originally intended to feed the hordes that would come off the buses—sorry, never happened. A small *loncheria* takes care of the inner man or woman.

A half-mile south of the gas station is the **Rancho Santa Inez,** a few hundred yards down a paved road to the left. The ranch offers several rooms ($; no phone), hot showers, camping, and excellent food. It's several notches up on the Pinta in terms of ambiance, romance, and all those indefinable qualities that make for good traveling.

A very bad dirt road (XXX) goes off for ten or so miles to the ruins of the last Jesuit-built mission, **Santa Maria de los Angeles.** It was resupplied from Bahia San Luis Gonzaga on the Sea of Cortez via a long-vanished trail. It must have been a hellish trek.

Mile 83 The **Rancho San Ignacito,** with a trucker's roadside restaurant, has its little footnote in history: a small monument on the west side commemorates the completion of the Transpeninsular Highway.

Mile 94 The road passes an old landmark, **El Pedregoso** (The Rocky Place), a pile of boulders just to the right of the road that goes up more than 3,000 feet above the distant sea. Several miles further on, the road comes out on the long run that passes on the west side of **Laguna Chapala.** Although this is a dry lake most of the time, it can have sticky mud beneath the crusty surface.

I once was coming up from the south, cresting the ridge that gave me an expansive view of the lake, when in the distance I saw what looked like a white ball, appearing and disappearing behind the chaparral that covers the edge of the lake. As I got closer, I realized that it was a helmeted rider about a hundred yards off the pavement, trying to drag his Honda Ascot twin back to the road. He was a young Japanese tourist who had rented the bike in Los Angeles and had been seduced by the notion of tearing across the lake bed, but after breaking through the thin crust, the mud had jammed up his front wheel good and proper. We pulled the bike to dry ground and got the mud out, and I sent him on his way. Be warned.

Mile 110 The turn for the dirt road (XX) to Gonzaga Bay and San Felipe (Chapter 8), as well as out to **Campo Calamajue** on the Sea of Cortez. On the right side is a *llantera* and *loncheria;* behind the buildings you'll find a dozen 55-gallon drums full of gas. They like to sell in ten-liter amounts, as this is the size of the can they use. The price will be about 25 percent higher than at a PEMEX, but I figure that into haulage. And don't worry about the gas being watered—the main clients are locals, and the gas merchants wouldn't be in business if they did that.

Mile 111 **Rancho Nuevo Chapala** is on the right, offering truck-stop food.

Five more miles and you are out of the Laguna Chapala valley and descending through an army of large **cardon cactus.**

Mile 127 Several abandoned buildings mark the beginning of **El Crucero** (The Cross), where a dirt road (XXX) on the left goes off 40 miles to the northeast to join with the Gonzaga road (Chapter 8). Sixteen miles along that road are the remains of the short-lived **Mision Calamajue;** lack of water doomed it early on.

Mile 141 The **Bahia de los Angeles turn-off** (Chapter 13), is often referred to as the **Punta Prieta junction,** though the actual village of PP is really a few miles farther on. There is an abandoned PEMEX on the right side, and a very large automotive junkyard on the left. And, there is often a benign military presence. Sometimes a local can be found at the defunct gas station with drums of gas in the back of his pickup; he is looking for the likes of you, and his markup might be a good deal higher than 25 percent.

Mile 150 The roadside community of **Punta Prieta** has food, both in cafe and grocery forms, and little else.

The road eases through some low hills, comes up on a ridge, and you can see a serious expanse of scrub and desert in front of you. This is the beginning of the great **Vizcaino Desert** which stretches for the next 130 miles.

Mile 165 A reasonably good dirt road (XX) goes west ten miles to the fish camp and surf spot at **Santa Rosalillita;** from there you can head north up the **Lost Coast** on some very bad roads indeed. I would suggest it only for lightweight D-Ps with big gas tanks, traveling in a group. It's lonely out there.

Mile 173 The village of **Rosarito** is off to the east of the road, and a failed PEMEX to the west. There are also signs to **Mision Borja** (see sidebar), some 23 miles down a dirt road (XX).

Mile 200 A rural PEMEX is to your left as you enter the village of **Villa Jesus Maria;** in my experience, this station has always had gas, supplied, as it is, from the south. The *tamale* stand by the road provides tasty food.

Fifteen more miles down the road, something large starts to loom on the horizon. What is it? A monolith? An abandoned skyscraper? A giant bird?

Mile 218 Just past the entrance to the **Guerrero Negro Airport** is the restaurant **La Espinita** (The Little Thorn), all by itself on the west side of the road—a clean, well-lighted place, open by 8 a.m. Local lore has it that in the bad old days this was a whorehouse and gambling den—since it was just north of the state line, it was legally immune from Baja California Sur intervention, and the Baja California (Norte) officals didn't much give a damn about what happened way down there. Now it is merely a good place to eat.

Mile 219 Yes, it is a giant bird, a modernistic, metallic interpretation of an **eagle,** standing about 140 feet tall. This statue marks the **28th parallel,** the division between Baja California (Norte) and Baja California Sur. Out in the middle of the desert, the

A Spritual Oasis

The sidetrip to San Borja is worth the time and effort. The road (XX) out goes through some marvelous red-soil country, with all manner of cacti, and leads to the middle of absolutely nowhere. The mission is a sight—large, restored stone edifice next to the remains of the 18th century adobe church. The hardpacked dirt square in front of the mission covers about an acre, and off to the side are a half a dozen little houses. Lady Maria Borja, the Duchess of Gandia, obviously felt that her soul was in danger, and gave a lot of money to the Jesuits to build some missions. When the Jesuits signed off on the place in 1767, they claimed 621 cattle, 1,108 sheep, 232 horses, 722 goats, and 1,618 Indian converts.

It is best to go back the way you came, but if you are very adept with a lightweight d-p, an exceptionally bad dirt road (XXX) goes north from the mission to meet the Bahia de los Angeles road (Chapter 13).

■

The mission at San Borja, 23 hard miles east of Mex 1 at Rosarito (Sur), is a splendid sight, but it makes one wonder why the padres went to all that work. Services are still held here.

The eagle is the symbol of Mexico, featured on the Mexican flag. This 140-foot high, highly stylized bird sits on the state line between Baja California (Norte) and Baja California Sur, at the 28th latitude north.

complex beneath and around the stylized eagle was supposed to be edifying to both the tourist and the student. However, as with many Baja ideas, the idea has fallen into limbo, and windows are broken and metal is rusting. There is a minor police and military presence, and an agricultural inspection station which ensures that no fruits or veggies come into BCS from the north.

There is the possibility of a **time change** here. BCS is an hour ahead of BC(N), but BCS does not recognize **Daylight Saving Time,** while BC(N) does. Which means that when BC(N) is on DST, there is no time change. Got that?

Just south is the **Hotel La Pinta** ($$; phone (115) 71305; U.S. 800-336-5454), with 28 rooms, a swimming pool, and a mandatory PEMEX pump, all out in the middle of not much.

Mile 221   The road forks, the left going on across the desert, the right into the charming (I joke) company town of **Guerrero Negro.** The name came from an American whaling ship, *Black Warrior,* that wrecked on this coast in 1858. The town of GN exists because the Exportadora de Sal S.A. (ESSA) exports about five million tons of salt from there every year. South of town, the sun evaporates salt water in more than 100 square miles of salt pans. The community, dependent on ESSA paychecks, stretches for some two skinny miles along Blvd. Emiliano Zapata.

A mile along Blvd. Emiliano Zapata, on the right, is the **Malarrimo Motel & Restaurant** ($$; phone (115) 70100), which offers full whale-watching services. Next is the **Hotel El Morro** ($$; phone (115) 70414) with a restaurant; they also arrange whale tours. My personal favorite, however, would be the ascetic **Motel Dunas** ($; phone (115) 70057), 50 *pesos* at last stay, with hot water after 6 p.m. This very monkish motel doesn't offer much more than a clean room, a clean bed, and a clean bathroom, but when I'm on the road I don't need frills like TV or badly done reproductions hanging on the wall. The Dunas has a supermarket on one side, and the **Restaurant El Figon** (mildly redundant, as a *figon* is a cheap restaurant) on the other; it is good, but it is not a fast-food place, and service can take a while.

Town itself is pretty minimal, with an uninspired collection of bars, cafes, stores, garages, and PEMEX stations. If you head on through town, keeping to your left as you pass over a small causeway, you will be on the five-mile dirt road (X) to the old wharf on **Laguna Guerrero Negro;** it is a nice ride, with a nice view, and **birdwatchers** might spot nearly 100 species in the area. A lucky few might even see a **grey whale** floating along in January or February.

That waterway became too shallow, and a new pier, closed to the public, opened up south of town near the entrance to **Scammon's Lagoon.** There the salt is put on barges and floated out about 65 miles to **Cedros Island,** where it is put on proper ships.

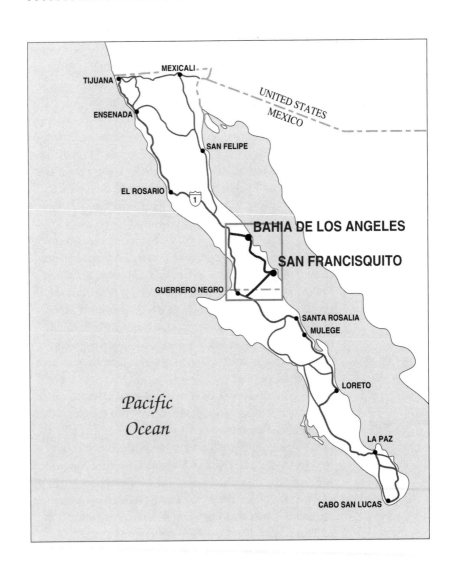

TIJUANA

MEXICALI

ENSENADA

UNITED STATES
MEXICO

SAN FELIPE

EL ROSARIO

BAHIA DE LOS ANGELES

SAN FRANCISQUITO

GUERRERO NEGRO

SANTA ROSALIA
MULEGE

LORETO

*Pacific
Ocean*

LA PAZ

CABO SAN LUCAS

13 Pavement & Dirt

· ·

Bahia de los Angeles might be the end destination of many *norteamericano* voyagers, but if you're not a fisherman, there's not all that much to do there. The place was only a small fishing village until the 1950s, when Papa Diaz built an airstrip and *gringo* anglers began to fly in. The motorhomes didn't show up until the Carreteria Transpeninsula opened.

For any motorcyclist in Baja, the trip down to the bay is a worthwhile detour. For those with a dual-purpose machine, it can be the start of something grand.

Let's see, you say we should be going this way, and I say we should be going that . . .
Kurt consults a map on the road between San Francisquito and El Arco.

The Road to Bahia de los Angeles

Distance   *42 miles*

Terrain   *The pavement is reasonably flat and straight (but of poor quality), getting a bit twisty in the last 10 miles as the descent to the coast becomes steeper.*

Highlights   *You'll get a nice view of the Isla Angel de la Guarda as you descend to the Bay of the Angels.*

Mile 0   Start on Mex 1 at the **Bahia de los Angeles junction.** Mex 1 continues south to Guerrero Negro, the other road goes east to Bahia de los Angeles.

At the junction is an abandoned (as of 1/97) PEMEX station on the west side of the road, and a huge junkyard to the south. A lot of vehicles have ended their useful lives in these here parts. Bored soldiers may be doing perfunctory vehicle searches.

It is 42 miles of crumbling, potholed pavement to the bay, so take it easy. The contractor obviously skimped on the asphalt. After many straightish miles of cruising alongside the **Sierra la Primavera** (Springtime Mountains), the road drops a bit.

Mile 28   A good-looking dirt road (XX) leads off to the right, the back way up to **Mision San Borja,** but do not be deceived; after a

Coming down the road, the first sight of the Bay of the Angels is downright beautiful.

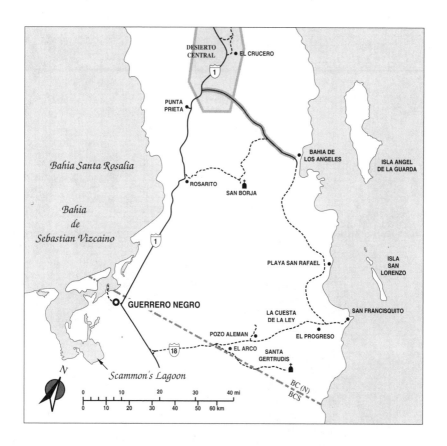

few miles it deteriorates severely, and you will wish you were on a DR350 with no baggage.

Mile 35 The road starts to descend toward the **Sea of Cortez,** and glorious views abound. If it is a sunny day, there will be a bit of glare off the essentially whitish rock around you. The sea will form a cobalt blue backdrop for the massive **Isla Angel de la Guarda** (Guardian Angel Island) just off the coast.

Mile 42 Main street in **Bahia de los Angeles** is loosely strung out for a mile, with several restaurants, motels and trailer parks. I stay at the old-fashioned one, **Casa Diaz** ($; phone (617) 86007; U.S. 619-278-9676), at the end of the street. Papa Diaz set up the place in the 1950s (long before there was a decent road) to lure American private pilots down for good fishing. The Diaz hotel has a dozen large, plain rooms, a big veranda, and a restaurant that is only occasionally open.

Down at Bahia de los Angeles, the official PEMEX *station may be closed, but at the adjacent Casa Diaz, the Diaz family always has some gasoline in barrels.*

The 40-room **Villa Vitti Hotel** ($$; phone U.S. 760-741-9583) is another option. If you want to be right on the beach, try one of the half dozen rooms at **Guillermo's Hotel** ($$; phone (665) 03206). Both of these establishments have restaurants. You can also eat at **Las Hamacas** on the main drag, a presentable restaurant serving breakfast, lunch and dinner.

In town, a small **museum** provides for an interesting hour. It is run by the expatriate American colony, and gives the viewer an appreciation of the ecological and geological riches of the area.

Down by the waterfront, in front of Casa Diaz is a PEMEX station which usually does not have any gas. Apparently the Diaz family and the gasoline distributor do not see eye to eye. Not to worry—a hundred yards to the south, by the boat and vehicle repair shop, the Diaz family has plenty of gas in barrels.

If you have a road-only motorcycle, go back to Mex 1 the way you came. If you have a dual-purpose bike, a good deal of stamina, and a 200-mile range, try the **San Francisquito** loop (XXX), which will put you back on Mex 1 a dozen miles south of Guerrero Negro (see next section this chapter).

Just remember, all it takes is an impassable 100 feet on a 100-mile road to screw everything up good and proper.

This poor old cow died of thirst in the boondocks, was propped up by some humor-minded locals, and now can serve to practice one's cape work.

To San Francisquito & Beyond

Distance   *122 dirt (XXX) miles*

Terrain   *Roll through coastal land until the road turns west to climb steeply up into the high country, before flattening into the desert.*

Highlights *Explore remote beaches, and get a close-up view of a fly-in resort, San Francsquito, gone to seed. The ride up the grade that rules, la Cuesta de la Ley, is thrilling.*

Mile 0   The dirt road from Bahia de los Angeles starts where the main street T-bones into Casa Diaz. Take a right, then a left, and the road heads south for 86 miles to **Bahia San Francisquito.** It was originally intended to be an excellent unpaved road which would attract motorized folk to the fly-in hotel at **San Francisquito,** and it represented a fine effort at road construction—properly graded, with concrete *vados* set in place. In 1992, however, a hurricane swept through and turned much of it to junk. Most of the road is still reasonably good, but in the places where the water poured out of the mountains, things got torn up badly, leaving the contemporary motorcyclist to struggle across soft-sand washes where the *vados* have been turned at right angles to the flow of water. Going can be rough enough to rate this road (XXX).

The road starts quite smoothly, passing by one of many mining operations that failed to make good. From 1889 to 1910, the San Juan Mining Company made a serious effort at extracting silver and a little gold. They even built a short railroad to take the ore to the sea where it could be loaded onto ships. It's all gone now.

Mile 46   The ride has been quite easy up to **Playa San Rafael,** where you can camp on the beach and not be troubled by any neighbors at all. After this, the road goes inland a bit; that's where the tough spots lie. Don't forget, it only takes 10 impassable yards to make the whole road useless.

Mile 74   This intersection is near the village of **El Progreso.** Take a left; the road heads out to the coast.

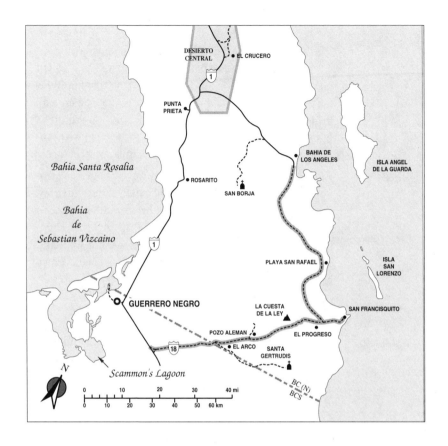

Mile 86   You have wound around some marshes and are at the **Punta San Francisquito Resort** ($$; no phone), with its own landing strip and occasional fuel. The rooms are in separate *palapa* huts, with a common bathroom; service can vary from rather ragged to quite good. Several houses owned by American pilots are also strung out along the beach, with their planes parked right on the strip.

When you leave, retrace your wheel marks back to El Progreso and continue straight toward the west, through absolutely stupendous cactus forests.

Mile 108   You are at the bottom of **La Cuesta de la Ley**—"The Grade Rules" is one translation, meaning that it is a minor hassle to get to the top. On a dry day, there should not be much of a problem. Some of the road is merely cleared-off rock with about a 15-degree outward slope, and other bits are full of loose stuff. A goodly degree of competence is in order, but if a fully loaded 1000cc dual-purpose bike can make it up . . .

As the road crosses a plateau you'll see a large rock corral off to one side, as well as other signs of ranching. When the narrow dirt road starts to wind and weave, you are on the brink of re-entering some sort of civilization. You'll pass quasi-abandoned mining operations at **Pozo Aleman** (German Well—to commemorate a German prospector).

Mile 138 **El Arco** (the Arch, the Rainbow, whatever) began as a gold-mining camp 70 years ago, but when the yellow stuff played out, more serious mining concerns began pulling copper ore out of the ground. An old church, a rustic repair shop, a hundred or fewer residents, and a detachment of soldiers are all that remain. Nevertheless, this is the social and economic hub—such as it is—for a number of ranches in the area.

Sidetrip For the **mission** collectors, Saint Gertrude's is 23 miles to the east, down a rough dirt road (XXX). **Santa Gertrudis** was begun by the Jesuits in 1752, finished by the Dominicans in 1796, and abandoned in 1822 due to lack of water and the fact that most of the converted locals had died of European diseases.

The old dirt road from Santa Rosalia to Guerrero Negro passed through El Arco many years ago, but now Mex 1 lies 26 miles to the east, connected by the grandiosely enumerated Mexico Highway 18. Although Mex 18 was once paved, the asphalt is so badly torn up now that it is painful to ride along; stick to the dirt roads on the sides.

Mile 164 When you come out on Mex 1, **Guerrero Negro** is 16 miles to the north, **Vizcaino Junction** 26 miles to the south. You are 96 miles farther south on Mex 1 from where you turned off to go to Bahia de Los Angeles.

Baja California Sur

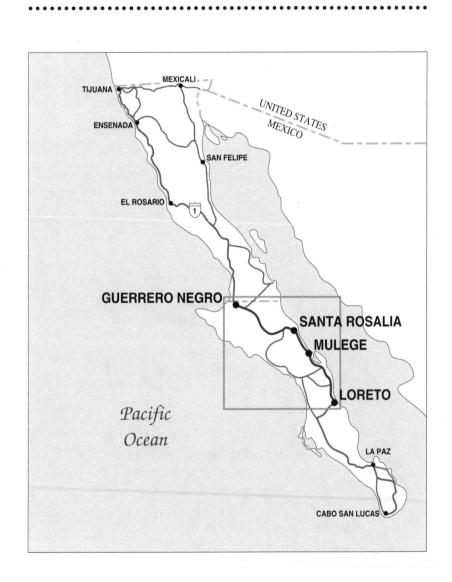

14 The Best Bit

This next stretch, by my humble reckoning, encompasses the best of Baja. Some people like the heavily touristed northernmost section, others prefer the southern Cabos. Me, I'll take the middle. It has stunning scenery, lots of history, and adventurous roads—everything a good traveler looks for.

The whale-watching boats at Scammon's Lagoon are controlled by the government, and it is best to make arrangements through one of the Guerrero Negro tourist offices; however, if you just show up at the beach, and there's room in a boat . . .

Guerrero Negro to Loreto on Mex 1

. . . .

Distance	*249 miles*
Terrain	*The road begins flat and fast through the desert, but changes into dips and curves as you cross over the Peninsula Divide, before descending steeply to the Sea of Cortez. South of Santa Rosalia the road curves gently southward, out of sight of (but usually not far from) the sea.*
Highlights	*Explore the town of San Ignacio, with a lagoon, a huge date grove, and a splendid old mission building in the town square. Santa Rosalia has Mr. Eiffel's prefabricated church and the picturesquely scattered detritus of a defunct mining town. The town of Mulege has charm and romance and good food. The first view of Bahia Concepcion is probably the most beautiful sight in Baja.*

Mile 0 Where the road from Guerrero Negro meets Mex 1 you're on the northwest edge of the **Vizcaino Desert,** which has now been ecologically labeled **El Vizcaino Biosphere Reserve.** About the Biosphere . . . the Mexicans are prone to designating an area as a natural wonder, having a great ceremony, and then forgetting all about it. I presume various Mexican universities go off and do academic things in these natural areas, but there is no information available to the public. I must admit, with over 5,000 square miles of desert and mountain covered by sand, rock, and cactus, the place does not appear to be useful for much besides mining and ranching.

On the whole, I find the desert delightfully inhospitable, because I am one who likes solitude.

If, however, a 40-mile-an-hour wind is blowing at right angles to the road, I might think otherwise about the delightful part.

Mile 6 There is the well-marked turn-off to the **Parque Natural de la Ballena Gris** (Grey Whale) 16 miles away. This is quite a little cash cow (whale variety) that is successfully milked. It's a two-star (XX) dirt road, generally good but with an occasional bit of blown sand that might hinder a Gold Wing rider who is not familiar with dealing with soft stuff.

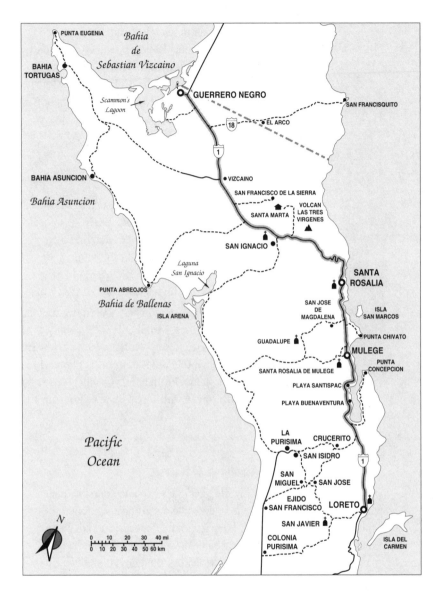

If you head out to the whale-watching area, you'll pay a nominal entry fee of 20 *pesos* ($3) at a small shed. To get there, you have to cut through a lot of the salt-making area; when in doubt (as the road to the viewing area is not well-marked), stay left. You'll end up on a beach on **Laguna Ojo de Liebra** (Hare's Eye Lagoon), popularly known, at least among Americans, as **Scammon's Lagoon.**

If you are at the lagoon in the winter months, you can see the **whales** from the shore. To be guaranteed a place in one of the licensed sight-seeing boats, arrange for it at one of the places in **Guerrero Negro,** the Malarrimo or Morro motels being the easiest (Chapter 12). However, if there is a boat going out that is not full, you may be able to just negotiate a price and have a look at these aquatic mammals at close quarters. How close? If you tip the boatman, close enough to stroke the barnacled back—although he is supposed to keep a respectful distance of a few feet.

Back on Mex 1, the road goes past the **El Arco** turn-off (Chapter 13) and travels headlong into the desert. As you cruise along at 100 mph on the generally straight, rarely trafficked, occasionally pot-holed two-laner, warning signs will state: PRECAUCION: NO ES UN CAMINO DE ALTA VELOCIDAD ("Warning: This is not a high speed road"). Fancy that.

Mile 44   The junction community of **Vizcaino** has PEMEX, two motels, a restaurant, and several stores. **Motel Olivia** ($; phone (115) 40024) is a reasonable place to stay, with the **Restaurant La Huerta** next door. **The Motel Kadakaaman** ($; phone (115) 40127) costs about the same. From here, you can take-off on the 109-mile paved, gravel, and dirt road that goes up the

---

He Made a Killing

Charlie Scammon was a whaling-ship captain who sailed into the quiet waters of the lagoon in 1857 and realized he had a fortune at hand. In those times people lighted their homes with oil lanterns, and whale oil was the primo stuff to burn. The whales, never having been molested by man, just floated around while the sailors slaughtered them to fill their cargo hold with barrels of this valuable commodity.

Scammon returned to San Francisco, laden to the gunwales, and aroused much curiosity as to how he had been so successful in such a short time. The crew was sworn to secrecy. Next year he returned to the lagoon and repeated the process, but this time he was followed, and the year after that other whalers appeared in droves and nearly wiped out the whale breeding grounds. So much for the nobility of man. ∎

middle of the **Peninsula de Vizcaino** to the fishing town of **Bahia Tortugas** (Turtle Bay) and to **Punta Eugenia.** From **Vizcaino Junction,** head south. Nothing dramatic, just a lot of old plastic bags and litter hung by the wind on the barbed-wire fences. Baja California may be moving into the consumer era, but the garbage collecting is still back in the Dark Ages.

The desert soil is not only dry, but saline, and only the hardiest of vegetation can survive: **creosote bushes,** and a lot of opportunistic **jumping cholla.**

Sidetrip   I've not been out on the Vizcaino peninsula myself, but have spoken to those who have. The 92 miles out to Turtle Bay are usually in relatively good condition: asphalt for the first 16 miles, then graded dirt (XX) which may suffer from mile after mile of washboard. Turtle Bay, a major yachting stop for Baja boaters, has a motel and a PEMEX. A softer road heads out to **Punta Eugenia,** and there is excellent **beach-combing** on the **Malarrimo beaches** on the north side of the peninsula.

If you don't wish to return to Vizcaino Junction by the same route, you can take slightly rougher dirt roads (XXX) down to **Bahia Asuncion** (Assumption Bay) and **Punta Abreojos** (Point Eye-Opener?), rejoining Mex 1, 28 miles south of Vizcaino Junction.

Mile 60   To the left is a turn to the village of **San Francisco de la Sierra.** I recommend this sidetrip (XX) for dual-purpose bikes. The 23 miles into the village are good, as the road climbs up on the eroded volcanic mesas to give you a view down into the **Cañon San Pablo.** Descending from the mountains, however, is even better, with a view directly across the Vizcaino Desert to the **Sierra Santa Clara** on the Pacific side (see sidebar next page).

Ars Gratis Artis

Near the village of San Francisco de la Sierra is the Cueva del Raton (Rat Cave), with some fine prehistoric cave paintings, including a 30-foot mural showing people, cougars and deer. It is all under lock and key, but up in the village you can find an government-approved guide to take you in. I promise you, it is a small village, so you won't have any problem locating a guide.

There are actually many caves with paintings in this central portion of Baja. The Jesuits noted their existence, but the first vaguely scholarly look was taken in 1894 by a Frenchman, Leon Diguet. Diguet wrote some learned words on this phenomenon, but once again the caves were half-forgotten until the 1960s, when the American mystery writer Earle Stanley Gardner developed quite an interest in this early art. Who these early Picassos were is anybody's guess, as the Cochimi Indians that were there during the early days of the Spanish colonization denied any shared lineage with these people. ∎

Mile 72   Go past the turn to Punta Abreojos, marked by the parked trucks at the **Crucero del Pacifico Restaurant.**

From here the road starts twisting a bit. At the 80-mile point, watch out for a deep *arroyo;* the approaches are steep on both sides, with turns, and the bottom collects its share of wrecks.

Mile 87   **San Ignacio** is off to your right—the most delightful town in Baja, by my humble estimation. When the *padres* came tromping through, a quarter-millenium ago, they found a steady supply of water in this little oasis, and decided the word of God could be spread more easily from reasonably comfortable surroundings. The mission, which claims to have been in continuous service, was begun by the Jesuits in 1728 and was finished by the Dominicans many years later.

The road into town goes past a small lagoon and a large grove of 80,000 date palms, and enters into a dusty *zocalo* (town square) with the **mission church** on the west side. A small **museum** with a good deal of information on the cave painters is off to the left side. The hours of the museum are a bit vague, but a caretaker can usually be found during morning and late afternoon hours. He can also tell you more about getting to the actual cave sites. If you need more assistance with organizing a trip to the caves, the Fischer family, owners of the Hotel La Posada, are very helpful.

Accommodation in town is either at the **Hotel La Pinta** ($$; phone (115) 40300; U.S. 800-336-5454), on the way in, or at the six-unit **Hotel La Posada de San Ignacio** (sort of redundant—"Hotel the Inn") for $20 a night ($; phone (115) 40013). La Posada is tucked away on an unpaved back street, but there aren't too many streets in San Ignacio so it is not difficult to find. It was built by a German sailor, Frank Fischer, who jumped ship in Santa Rosalia about 1900 and moved up to San Ignacio. His descendants still own the place. Nearby is the **Restaurant Totas,** with commendable food. Another good place to eat is **Rene's Bar,** close by the town square, where both locals and tourists mingle.

If you keep on past the Restaurant Totas, the rough road will eventually lead to **Laguna San Ignacio,** and points south—but we will deal with that in Chapter 20.

Back on the highway at Mile 97, there is a PEMEX at the junction. Soon you are crossing over the mountain range which runs the length of Baja, and start descending to the **Sea of Cortez** side.

Mile 106   The dirt road (XX) to **Rancho Santa Marta** goes off to the left; this place, 28 miles off the highway, is often used as a jumping-off point for exploring some of the painted caves. The hospitable folk at the ranch can even rustle up some horses and a guide to take you out, after which you will understand the true meaning of "saddle sore."

Who was this guy Vizcaino?

Old Sebastian V. was a Spanish explorer who founded La Paz in 1596, and later sailed up the coast of California as far as Monterey Bay, which he named. As a result of all that, his own name got attached to much of Baja . . . though admittedly not the best part.

■

Climbing up into the Sierra San Francisco, one can look back across the Vizcaino Desert to the often fog-shrouded Pacific coast.

To the north of Mex 1 are the **Volcan Las Tres Virgenes** (Three Virgins Volcano), three distinct peaks on the horizon. The tallest one is 6,299 feet. Although they're not very active, they do provide the heat for a geothermal power project a little to the east. Watch the descent, as the corners should be taken seriously. If you want to admire the ocean views, stop.

Mile 139   You are entering **Santa Rosalia,** a most charming (if somewhat scruffy) town. It is a **ferry terminal** for those wanting to cross the Sea of Cortez to **Guaymas** on the mainland—but you'd better have your paperwork in order (see Chapter 2).

As you go along the waterfront, everything is covered in a dingy brown residue from more than 100 years of mining and smelting. It's a working town, not a vacation spot. A shabby park is home to a collection of mining equipment, though the casual passerby might think it was a junkyard.

Mining concerns first found copper deposits in the 1860s. The ore came naturally in little balls of copper carbonate and oxides, hence the name of the Compagnie de Boleo, the French outfit that moved in to exploit this resource in 1885. The French bailed in 1954, and the work was taken over by a Mexican operation until it shut down in 1990.

The French connection explains why the town church, **Santa Barbara,** is a metal pre-fab structure designed by A. G. Eiffel (of Eiffel Tower fame). The church was originally set up at the Paris World Fair of 1889, and was sent to Baja in pieces about a hundred years ago.

Mile 141   A little locomotive sits in a small square to the right. The town proper is in an *arroyo* between two mesas, a skinny 30 blocks with a bank, a bakery, and all the merchandise you could hope for. I discovered great *tacos* at the outdoor stand on Avenida Alvaro Obregon, just a few doors down from the bank.

If you wish to spend the night here, you have several choices. Up on the north mesa above the town proper is the reconditioned **Hotel Frances** ($, maybe $$; phone (115) 20829), an old wooden structure built to house visiting company executives. At the south end of town, past the PEMEX station, is the **Motel El Morro** ($$; phone (115)

20414), catering to the ferry crowd and to big wedding parties (you do not want to stay in a motel where a large Mexican wedding is taking place, because local social gatherings tend to be extremely noisy and extend into the wee hours). In town itself, toward the west end of the *arroyo* at Avenida Progreso 36, is the clean and neat **Motel San Victor** ($; (115) 20177).

Continuing south, the road pulls away from the sea, goes by a state prison (if that view of the austere, isolated, baking-hot penitentiary wouldn't keep a potential criminal on the straight and narrow, nothing will), affords a glimpse of **San Marcos Island,** and then heads inland skirting **Punta Chivato** (Young Goat Point). A long, unused airstrip is just a mile off the road, one of those government projects which never went anywhere.

Mile 157   A spectacular, well-marked dirt road (XXX, just to be on the conservative side of safe) heads west 70 miles to **San Jose de Magdalena** and loops back down to Mulege.

Sidetrip   The loop from **Mulege** to **San Jose de Magdelena** is a relatively easy (XX) road, *except* for one difficult (XXX) bit. It's nine good miles to **San Jose.** Five miles beyond San Jose, you stay to the left and enter a dark canyon where the road begins a serious climb with lots of loose stones; it is a tough stretch. At the top, it immediately starts an equally steep run down—not for the faint of heart. Beyond that, the road flattens out into a lovely valley, where you'll find the remains of the foundation of the **Mision Guadalupe** (established in 1721, abandoned in 1795). From here you can maintain a goodly speed on hard-packed dirt. Fifteen miles south of the ruins at a small ranch you'll see a turn off to the right, the **Raymundo Road,** 41 extremely rough (XXX) miles that go along the **Arroyo San Raymundo** to meet up with the **West Side Highway** (Chapter 12). Stay straight, and you will arrive in Mulege just north of the bridge.

Mile 165   A good 12-mile gravel road (XX) will run you out to the **Punta Chivato Resort Hotel,** ($$; phone (115) 30188) with great sunsets, great fishing, and all that—the only problems lie with the quality of service at the hotel itself. An American originally made a deal with the local *ejido* to develop the place, but several years ago, after the work had been done and the place was getting a name for itself, the *ejido* threw out the American and took it over. Where things stand remains unsettled.

Climb through a few hills, and the road descends into the valley of the **Rio Santa Rosalia.**

Mile 177   There are houses on both sides of the road, a bridge ahead, and a turn into town on the left. Nice place. Up river is the old **Mision Santa Rosalia de Mulege** (1705) , and on top of the hill is the old prison which has been brilliantely whitewashed and converted into a **museum**— a captive of the church or a captive of the state, take your pick. The prison/museum, run by volunteers, is ostensibly open from 9:00 to 1:00 daily, but if you find it closed, any child in the area will be happy to run off and locate somebody with a key.

Mulege is tucked along the north shore of the "only navigable" river in Baja, and that is just for half a mile at high tide; the river's official name is **Rio Santa Rosalia,** but most people refer to it as **Rio Mulege.** There is a small *zocalo* with the Hotel Hacienda on one side and a supermarket on another.

The best fish *tacos* in Baja (by my own unprejudiced opinion) are sold from a tiny shanty on wheels between 8 and 11 a.m. My friend and riding companion, Kurt, who lived in Mulege in the mid-1970s, once asked the fellow why he didn't keep longer hours. The vendor responded, "I make enough money this way to be happy; why should I work more than I have to?" Which pretty much defines an attitude you'll find in much of Mexico. In spite of this, gas stations function well, rural motels and restaurants always have someone on the premises, and down in the TZs, the employees are getting positively efficient; it is only in the local-local world that you will see remnants of this philosophy.

At the other end of the spectrum of financial thinking is the **Mulege Dive Shop** (phone (115) 30059) on Avenida Martinez, a block down from the PEMEX station. The owners (Miguel is Mexican, Claudia, American) know the very best places to go snorkeling or SCUBA diving in the magnificent waters of the Sea of Cortez, whether you want a half day, full day, or over-nighter. The diving equipment is kept to the highest standards. They have good maps of the area (both have dual-purpose bikes), and as a new sideline they also rent **mountain bikes,** which are always an interesting temporary alternative to motor bikes.

The **Hotel Hacienda** ($; phone (115) 30021) is a low-bucks affair, built as a traditional wealthy family's house 100 years ago, with a courtyard inside. It became a counterculture (read: hippie) hotel in the 1960s, and has maintained a little bit of that carefree air. There is a fenced-in parking area, but if you are paranoid, you can push your bike into the courtyard. I like the place, except that there is a bar in the courtyard, and since all the rooms face inward, it can get a trifle noisy.

The **Hotel Terrazas** ($; phone (115) 30009) on Calle Zaragoza is also available, as is the small **Hotel Las Casitas** ($$; phone (115) 30019) at Calle Madero 50, with an excellent restaurant.

The south side of the river is basically Gringoland, with houses and trailers along the banks. Down toward the mouth of the river is the pleasant **Hotel Serenidad** ($$; phone (115) 30530), complete with its own airstrip and a pig roast on Saturday nights. In late 1996, it too was undergoing some problems with the local *ejido,* but we can only hope at this writing that it is functioning at its usual high standards.

For dining, the Serenidad is good, as are the downtown eateries (with only 5000 inhabitants, Mulege does not have a very extensive downtown). **Los Equipales,** a second-story restaurant on Calle Moctezuma, has a nice verandah for open-air breakfasting or dining, but the best place of all is out on the beach. If you take the dirt road along the north side of the river all the way to the end, where a hillock stands with a lighthouse atop, you will see a *palapa* building to the north which houses **El Sombrerito** restaurant. It's positively the most romantic place in Baja—and the food is good, too.

Mile 179 Two miles south of town is a large PEMEX, a small grocery store, and a place to send and receive faxes—the modern world has come to Mulege. But the road goes on, slips into a few hills, and comes out to the most beautiful sight: **Bahia Concepcion.** The bay, bounded on the far side by a mountainous peninsula, is almost 25 miles long and three to five miles wide. It is a haven for sailors and motorhomers, and the beaches are often cluttered with *palapas* and Winnebagos.

Mile 190 You are at **Playa Santispac.** If you are in camping mode, ask the chap at the gate for a *palapa,* which runs maybe $5; you can buy food and water at the two little restaurants which serve the residents.

On the beach is a **kayaking** concern called **Baja Tropicales** ((115) 30190; U.S. 619-275-4225), run by Becky and

If you want to go out to Punta Concepcion, at the end of the peninsula on the east side of Conception Bay, you'll have to travel along some beaches, but it is a great trip for a dual-purpose bike.

Roy; they will teach you the basics of keeping a kayak going in the right direction, and send or take you out on a most splendiferous trip through the bay. The water is calm and clear, so the paddling is easy and the snorkeling is great. Prices are very reasonable: the all-day tour (highly recommended) is $39, meals included.

There are several other beaches along the way, but they can all get overcrowded. The road along the west side of the bay, however, is a brilliant ride.

Mile 202   A relatively new tourist complex, **George's Ole,** has been built by an American entrepreneur down at the south end of **Playa Buenaventura.** It features a motel ($$; phone (115) 30408), restaurant, satellite TV, and all the amenities.

Mile 204   An unmarked dirt road drops down to the left, goes past some semi-abandoned buildings, and loops around the bottom of the bay and up the far side through a huge forest of **cardon cactus.** From there, the road runs past an old fish camp and up into relative wilderness—take a lot of water with you, just in case. I'll give this an (XX) for difficulty, unless you try to get all the way to **Punta Concepcion** at the northern tip of the peninsula, in which case your off-road riding skills should be properly honed.

Mile 222   A pretty good, dead-straight dirt road (XX), well marked as SAN ISIDRO, goes off for 36 miles to the west (your right) to **La Purisma/San Isidro** and will connect you to the old **West Side Highway** (Chapter 20). Ridden with caution and experience, an FLH can easily make it.

Mex 1 tears south over rocky, brushy landscape, with nothing but an occasional abandoned store or scrawny cow to indicate the presence of people.

Mile 249   Here you are in **Loreto,** the first Spanish settlement in the Californias, founded in 1697 by Padre Salvatierra (Father Save-the-Earth). Mex 1 skirts the city, and at the obvious sign at Loreto Junction you will turn east. As you come down the avenue, a PEMEX will be on your left, and on the right the rather basic **Motel Salvatierra** ($; phone (113) 50021).

Loreto was the capital of Spanish Baja until the place got thumped good and proper by the hurricane of 1829. That, plus some politicking, got the seat of government

. . . Okay, Just One More . . .

I'll include one more excellent adventure in this section. Back on Mex 1 at the **Loreto Junction,** go half a mile south where a well-marked dirt road (XX) goes off to San Javier and the two Comondu villages, **San Jose** and **San Miguel.** After 16 miles of mildly mountainous meandering, the road forks, the right going 25 more miles to the Comondus, the left five miles to **San Javier.**

The Comondus are a delight because they are situated in a long *arroyo* that has lots of water. After the dry hills, you find yourself down in the green of date palms, sugar cane, fruits, and vegetables. San Jose has an old **mission** building now serving as the community church. Gas is usually available from a barrel at a rustic store in San Miguel.

From the Comondus you can go northwest to **La Purisima/San Isidro,** or southwest to **Ejido San Francisco** on the West Side Highway. Do *not* take the northerly road to **Palo Verde** and **El Crucerito**—I have it on the best opinion that it is one of the worst roads in Baja.

Back at the fork, go left and shortly you are in a most wonderful little village, with the superbly (I love those maximizing adjectives, and this one is appropriate) preserved mission of **San Francisco Javier de Vigge-Biaundo.** This was the second mission site in Baja, begun in 1699 because the little valley had good water, good grazing, and good earth (nothing would grow in the sandy Loreto soil).

From San Javier you can choose to go back to Mex 1, or continue on 44 miles to **Colonia Purisima** on the West Side Highway.

■

A superb dirt-road trip into the Sierra de La Giganta ends at the old mission at San Javier, some 25 miles southwest of Loreto.

moved to **La Paz.** To add insult to injury, Loreto was flattened by an earthquake in 1877—not that you would know it today. The **mission** has been rebuilt, the city looks clean, and the *malecon* (sea wall) is a delight to stroll along. A small fishing fleet still docks along the *embarcadero,* but mostly the harbor looks for rich people on pleasure boats. Not many come.

Look way north along the shore to spot a small white building among the palms along the beach. In the best tradition of sea-faring towns, it is a house of ill repute. Or so I've been told.

Any number of hotels are available, as Loreto once aspired to be Baja California Sur's tourist mecca. But, shortly after a major resort hotel was built, the Mexican government became interested in developing the Cabos, and Loreto has receded into a mild backwater. The **airport** is

Conception Bay is a most attractive place, even though the norteamericanos seeking southern sun seem to have cluttered up the beaches a fair bit, like here at Playa Santispac.

ostensibly an international one, but only two flights a day come in, not enough to support a major tourist economy.

The **Hotel La Pinta** ($$; phone (113) 50025; U.S. 800-336-5454) is down by the *malecon,* (sea wall) not far from the city center. **Hotel Oasis** ($$; phone (113) 50211) is also on the shore, half a mile south of the mission. Just across the *malecon,* at Ave. Lopez Mateos 1 is the **Hotel Mision de Loreto** ($$; phone (113) 50048), quite new and nice. Eight miles south of town, at **Nopolo,** where the big resorts were going to be, is the **Loreto Inn Hotel El Cortes** ($$$; phone (113) 30700; U.S. 310-943-6233), offering everything from diving trips to golf.

Food is all around. **Cafe Ole,** right on the plaza east of the mission, is good morning and afternoon, and **Cesar's,** two blocks west of the church at the corner of Zapata and Juarez streets, is good afternoon and evening.

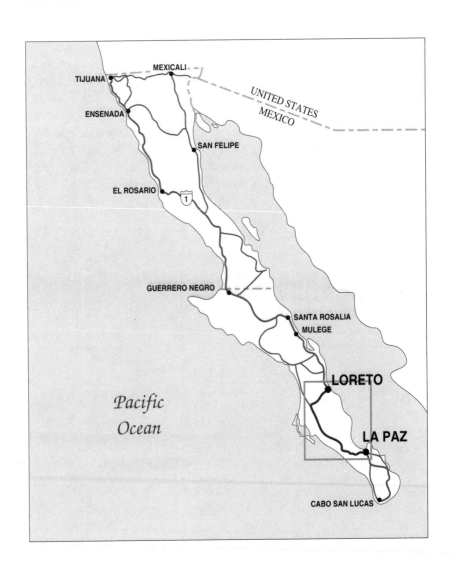

15 The Sierra de la Giganta

This is not a terribly stimulating stretch of highway. There are a few scenic views as you go down along the Sea of Cortez, but once away from the sea and in the middle of the peninsula, it can get a bit tedious. Until you approach La Paz.

Kids are kids all over the world, and they do love to look at motorcycles.

Loreto to La Paz on Mex 1

· ·

Distance *217 miles*

Terrain *This route begins along the coast, then climbs out over the Sierra de La Giganta to the flat plain of Llano de Magdalena, to cross back over the southern foothills of the Sierra de la Giganta to Bahia de La Paz.*

Highlights *Not many on this stretch, though the first views of the Bay of La Paz are rather nice.*

Mile 0 Gas up in Loreto at the PEMEX opposite the Motel Salvatierra and head out to the **Loreto Junction,** where Paseo Ugarte, the main road out of town, meets Mex 1. Follow Mex 1 past the San Javier turn-off (Chapter 14). A little beyond that is the left turn to the **airport**; the two or three flights a day bring in only an anemic supply of tourists.

Mile 5 A fancy road goes off to the left to **Nopolo,** the "tourist zone." In the 1970s this was supposed to be a "major" tourist zone, but politics got in the way, somebody else got into power, and the resort idea more or less fell apart. The **Loreto Inn** (Chapter 14) is, nonetheless, a very fancy hotel, with 250 rooms, a golf course, etc.

Mile 15 The turn to the left heads to **Puerto Escondido,** which was to be part of this great tourist complex. It has a beautiful natural harbor, which man has tried to improve upon without doing very well. It does have a good yacht basin and an RV park with a restaurant, but it ain't much . . . though more development is promised. Promises, promises.

Mile 22 The road starts climbing up into the **Sierra de la Giganta,** offering one last view of the **Sea of Cortez.**

Mile 35 A dirt road (XX) to the left runs 25 miles down to the fishing village of **Puerto Agua Verde.** It's a rugged trip, favored mostly by *gringo* sportsmen who set up camp down there to fish their little hearts out.

Mex 1 drops down a little out of the mountains to the plateau called **Llano de Magdelena** (Magdalena Plain),

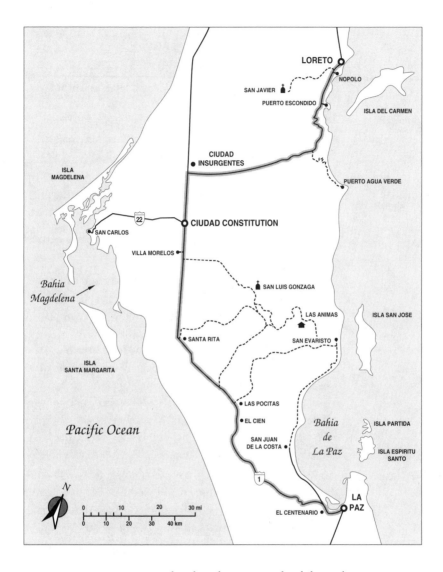

passes an abandoned PEMEX on the right, and comes
through cotton country.

Mile 73   This is the southern end of **Ciudad Insurgentes** (Rebel City).
The highway goes left (south) but if you need gas, turn right
on the main street of Ciudad Insurgentes and a PEMEX is 300
yards up on your left.

Mile 90   Entering **Ciudad Constitucion,** a major farming community
atop a gigantic aquafer. Cotton, wheat, vegetables, and fruit

all grow thanks to the presence of the non-renewable water resource.

The city has two PEMEX stations and a charming hostelry, **Manfred's RV Park & Austrian Restaurant** ($$), on the left as you enter town. Manfred is from Graz, Austria, and how he, and his elegant wife, ended up here is anybody's bet. They have several rooms available and excellent wienerschnitzel.

Mile 91   A long, straight, two-lane paved road, Mex 22, goes west for 35 miles to the port of **San Carlos** on **Bahia Magadalena.** It is an unromantic port town with a big pier, a fish cannery, and a lot of dirt, dust, and filthy water. Several small hotels, one suitably named the **Alcatraz,** cater to businessmen and sailors.

You are now entering the main part of Ciudad Constitucion, which has a half a dozen hotels for the business types. If you need accommodations, follow the signs on Mex 1 to the **Hotel El Conquistador** ($; phone (113) 21515) on Calle Nicolas Bravo, or the **Hotel Maribel** ($; phone (113) 20155) on Calle Guadalupe Victoria, both just east of the highway.

Constitution City also has every American name known to farming: John Deere, Dodge, Massey Ferguson, Chevrolet, the lot. But, in spite of this, CC is not what I would call a tourist destination.

Mile 101   Just after **Villa Morelos,** a dirt road (XX) goes east 24 miles to **Mision San Luis Gonzaga,** a site that was most active from 1751 to 1769. The restored mission sits above a small oasis, with palm trees fluttering over a pond. Very nice. Though the road deteriorates (XXX) past this point, it could take you either to the Sea of Cortez or back to Mex 1.

Mile 123   After 50 dead-straight miles you come into the village of **Santa Rita,** where the road makes a 30-degree turn to the left.

Mile 150   The village of **Las Pocitas,** notable only for its blacksmith. "Under the spreading oak the village smithy stands . . ." except here *el herrero* stands under a palm-fronded *palapa* and turns old automobile springs and what-not into bridle bits and spurs. He also sells knives made by another smith out at the **Rancho Las Animas,** 40 hard miles away to the north-

El herrero (the blacksmith) in Las Pocitas creates his bridle bits and spurs the old-fashioned way, with forge, anvil, hammer, and skill.

east; this is genuine craftsmanship. To find *el herrero*, look for the dirt road going left at the only intersection in the village, then back up along the highway three houses. Confusing? Slightly, but that is the way to find the smith; you will recognize his small workshop, and if he is not there, go over to the house.

Mile 159   A community called **El Cien** (The Hundred—just 100 km from La Paz), with a PEMEX.

Now you begin crossing back over the southern end of the **Sierra de la Giganta,** heading for the Sea of Cortez. You'll be able to glimpse the **Bay of La Paz.**

Mile 208   A paved road cuts back to the left, going up along the coast 24 miles to the mining town of **San Juan La Costa** (no precious metals, just phosphorus). Beyond La Costa a dirt road (XX) continues up the coast for another 44 miles to the fishing village of **San Evaristo,** opposite the **Isla San Jose.** From San Evaristo a very bad road (XXX) climbs through the **Sierra de la Giganta** and eventually joins with Mex 1.

Mile 209   The growing town of **El Centenario** has a PEMEX and other amenities.

Mile 213   The paved road to the right goes to **La Paz International Airport.**

Mile 214   Another huge statue in the middle of the road; the Bajaeneos love this statue stuff. At first look you think it is a whale's tail, but on closer inspection you realize it is the **Dove of Peace.** Here the road divides, the right heading down to Cabo San Lucas, the left going into **La Paz;** go left, and the road turns into Ave. Abasolo.

Mile 217   You are at the PEMEX station at the corner of Abasolo and 5 Febrero. Going forward takes you into the city proper. Taking a right on 5 Febrero would point you toward the Cabos.

This whale tail—or is it a dove of peace (paz)?—greets the traveler arriving at La Paz.

Cityscape La Paz

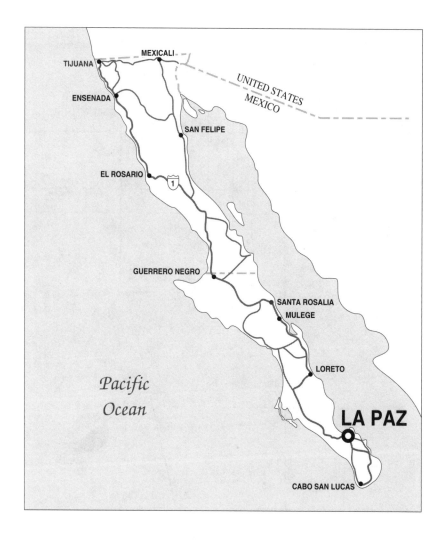

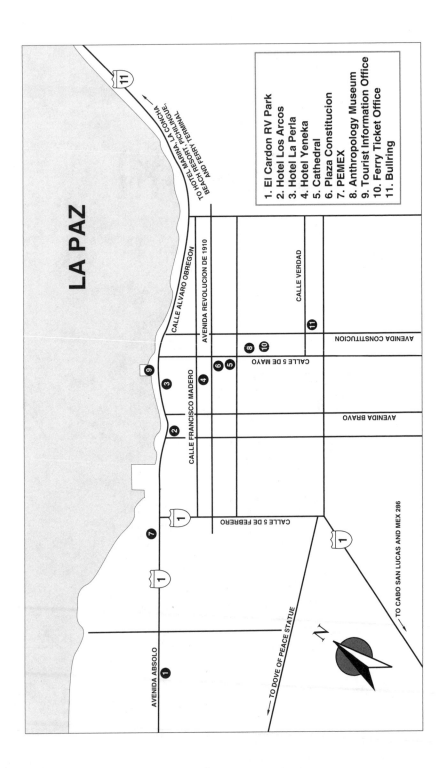

LA PAZ

1. El Cardon RV Park
2. Hotel Los Arcos
3. Hotel La Perla
4. Hotel Yeneka
5. Cathedral
6. Plaza Constitucion
7. PEMEX
8. Anthropology Museum
9. Tourist Information Office
10. Ferry Ticket Office
11. Bullring

TO HOTEL MARINA, LA CONCHA, LA CONGUE, PICHILINGUE, BEACH RESORT, AND FERRY TERMINAL

CALLE ALVARO OBREGON

AVENIDA REVOLUCION DE 1910

CALLE FRANCISCO MADERO

CALLE 5 DE MAYO

CALLE VERDAD

AVENIDA CONSTITUCION

AVENIDA BRAVO

CALLE 5 DE FEBRERO

AVENIDA ABSOLO

TO DOVE OF PEACE STATUE

TO CABO SAN LUCAS AND MEX 286

N

16 True City, and Nice, Too

Big place, **La Paz,** with over 100,000 peaceful types (bad pun: *paz* means peace). It's the capital of Baja California Sur and it has everything: a little bit of industry, a lot of service, a big bureaucracy, a university, etc. Even though it's in a beautiful location, the tourist business has remained very low-key. I'd say, of all the cities in Baja, La Paz is the most pleasant and the most genuine.

Five hundred years ago, some cheerful, well-fed Indians lived on this large bay, catching fish and game, and harvesting a few fruits and veggies from the wild (I may be exercising a little poetic license here, but early European reports did indicate that the natives had it quite good). Beginning in the early 16th century, the locals had intermittent contact with the disease-ridden Europeans, and the results were not always pleasant.

To catch a boat to the mainland, go a few miles northeast of town to the ferry terminal at Pichilingue; just make sure your paperwork is in order.

The view out to the Bay of La Paz is indeed peaceful.

Around 1720 the Jesuits established a mission, **Nuestra Señora Pilar de la Paz,** on the south shore of the bay, but the Indians had grown wary of the white-faces. The *padres,* in the face of indigenous hostility, moved the mission headquarters south to San Jose del Cabo in 1749. But, since the **Bay of Peace** provided safe mooring, Spanish fishermen and ranchers continued to use the place, building up the community of La Paz in the early 1800s.

One man's disaster is another man's fortune: when Loreto got smashed by a hurricane in 1829, the capitol of the territory was moved to La Paz. Ha! Politics had arrived.

After the Mexican-American War started in 1846, U.S. troops arrived and stayed until the **Treaty of Hidalgo** in 1848 divided Baja and Alta California up by the Tijuana River. La Paz retreated into somnolence.

A regular **ferry** service was inaugurated about 100 years later, connecting the city with the mainland. The **airplane** really woke the place up, and in the 1950s La Paz acquired a certain cachet amongst wealthy *norteamericano* fishermen. It was not until 1973, however, following the completion of the **Carretera Transpeninsula** and the subsequent development of the Cabos, that La Paz came into its own. BCS acquired Mexican statehood in 1974.

Today it's a big city, with roads and ships and airplanes connecting with the rest of Mexico and the world. La Paz also attracts lots of tourists, although those from mainland Mexico outnumber *gringos* three to one.

The main **BCS Tourist Office,** part of the Secretaria de Turismo (SECTUR), is out on Mex 1 (Ave. Abasolo) between km 5 and 6. The branch office is much more convenient, located on the pier on the *malecon,* just up from the Hotel La Perla (phone (112) 27676). Both are officially open from 8:00 in the morning to 7:00 in the evening, but if nobody is there, try again later.

If you have your paperwork, including the TVIP, in order (see Chapter 2), and want to take the ferry over to the mainland, you can go directly to the SEMATUR ferry company offices (phone (112) 53833) at the corner of Calles 5 de Mayo and Guillermo Prieto.

As you ride past the **Dove of Peace Monument** on Mex 1 (Chapter 15), the road turns into Ave. Abasolo and will lead right into the city, past the cheerful **El Cardon Trailer Park,** (phone (112) 40078) which offers camping, a swimming pool, and laundry facilities. Continue past the PEMEX at the corner of Calle 5 de Febrero (the road to take to continue on Mex 1 going south to Cabo), proceed straight to merge with the Calle Alvaro Obregon, and thence onto the waterfront and tourist office on the pier in the center of town.

This is where the action is. I recommend you stay at the **Hotel La Perla** ($$; phone (112) 2-0777; fax 5-5363), which has a very safe underground garage; it is right on the *malecon,* and its restaurant, **La Terrazza,** is the place to see and be seen. On the upscale side is the **Hotel Los Arcos** ($$$; phone (112) 2-2744; fax 5-4313; U.S. 800-347-2252) on Paseo Alvaro Obregon, about six blocks west of La Perla; the original hotel was built back in 1954, and newer bits have been added on.

Definitely downscale, but oh so delightfully funky, is the **Hotel Yeneka** ($; phone (112) 5-4688) on Calle Francisco Madero, three blocks behind La Perla, and one block from Plaza Constitucion; this is a place right out of the counterculture, and is popular with backpack travelers. If all you need is a clean room and running water, this is it. You can push your bike right into the crowded courtyard. The restaurant is excellent.

A bit of history and culture is in order: the **Catedral de Nuestra Señora de La Paz,** built in 1861, is on the southish side of **Plaza Constitucion.** Just to keep the chain of command defined, a church becomes a cathedral when there is a bishop around. Opposite the cathedral is the old governor's residence, now the **Biblioteca de Historia de las Californias,** open to the public, where the academically inclined can research the history of Baja and Alta California.

Five blocks south of the *zocalo,* at the corner of Calles Ignacio Altamirano and 5 de Mayo, is the **Museo Antropologico de Baja California Sur.** The museum is packed full of local history, geology, fauna, and flora, and is open

The cathedral of Nuestra Señora de la Paz, built in 1861 to replace the old church, fronts the downtown zocalo, or town plaza, of La Paz.

Tuesday through Friday from 8:00 to 6:00 and Saturday from 9:00 to 2:00. For a current socio-anthropological overview of life in La Paz, go to the **central market** at the corner of Degollado and Revolucion.

Like any proud Mexican city, La Paz has a **bullring**, at Ave. Constitucion and Primo Verdad. The *corridas* are usually held in February and March; details are available from the tourist bureau on the *malecon*.

Should you be having problems with your motorcycle, there are two motorcycle repair shops in town. The first, **Motor Sport,** is on Calle Rosales between Calle Heroes de la Independencia (not to be confused with Avenida Independencia) and Calle Gomez Farias. Luis Garcia, the head mechanic, speaks tolerable English (phone (112) 56423). The second, the **Vehiculos Deportivos Acuario** (Sport Vehicle Shop) is on Ave. Isabel la Catolica between Reforma and 16 de Septiembre (phone (112) 34037); owner Juan Landazuri also has a bit of English at his disposal. Neither of these generic fix-it shops have much in the way of spare parts, but if they can't repair what is ailing your machine, they can order the part from Mexico City and have it FedExed in (or the local equivalent).

Sidetrip   If you have your paperwork done to take the ferry to the mainland, or want to go out on the beaches on the pensinsula that protects the Bay of La Paz, follow your nose, or front wheel, along the *malecon* and go right through La Paz, coming out the north side on Mex 11, which leads up to the **Pichilingue ferry terminal** 10 miles north. On the way you'll pass two big resorts, **La Concha Beach Resort** ($$$; phone (112) 2-6544; U.S. 800-999-2252) on Playa Ciamancito, and the **Marina Hotel** ($$$; phone (112) 2-6254; fax 2-6277; U.S. 800-826-1138) located next to a large marina that serves the many yachts that cruise these waters. Both are a long way, however, from the fun of downtown.

*This beaming boy is happy because his folks run the taco stand by the La Paz market,
and he gets all the tacos he wants*

About five miles beyond the ferry terminal, the pavement ends at **Playa Tecolote,** where two restaurants, **El Tecolote** and **Palapa Azul,** compete for the customers. The seafood is fresh, and the oysters are delicious. A dirt road (XX) goes another few miles farther to **Playa Coyote,** but the sand along this road has the texture of talcum powder, so be prepared.

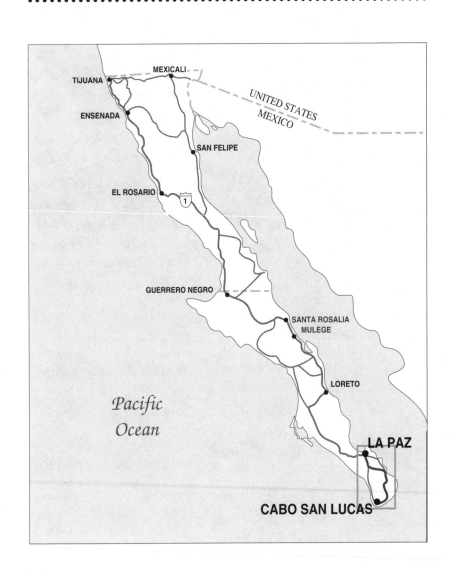

17 The Final Dash

Get back to the PEMEX at the corner of Abasolo and 5 de Febrero in La Paz (Chapter 16). I know this urban mapping is a misery, but you gotta do what you gotta do.

Mexico Highway 1 is coming to the end of its 1,060 miles; Land's End can be seen in the distance.

La Paz to Cabo San Lucas on Mex 1

· ·

Distance *133 miles*

Terrain *After crossing the flat Llano de la Paz the road starts some semi-serious twisting to wind through the Sierra de La Laguna, to emerge at Bahia de Palmas. The road then skirts the Sierra de la Laguna, with gentle curves, and turns into the four-lane highway which runs along the sea between the two Cabos.*

Highlights *Explore the old mining center of El Triunfo. Celebrate your crossing into the Tropic of Cancer. San Jose in San Jose del Cabo provides a pleasing window into Mexican life. And, of course, Cabo San Lucas awaits you at the end of the road.*

Mile 0 Head south on Ave. 5 de Febrero for 15 blocks; don't bother counting the blocks, unless you enjoy the precision, because your turn to find Mex 1 and Cabo San Lucas comes after a largish open area housing a **sports complex** on your right, with a soccer field, and courts for basketball and volleyball. The road angles off to the right at 45 degrees rather than 90.

Mile 1 Make that 45-degree turn. The **Carretera al Sur,** officially known as **Blvd. Forjadores,** is large and well-marked, with signs pointing the way toward Cabo San Lucas. There is a **youth hostel** ($; phone (112) 24615) at the corner of Blvd. Forjadores and Calle 5 de Febrero. The rooms each have four beds, and a night costs about $4, $3 if you are a member of the American Youth Hostel Association (phone U.S. (202) 763-6161).

Mile 1+ The way to Mex 1 is straight, but a well-marked turn to the left goes to **San Juan de los Planes** on State Highway 286 (see sidebar overleaf).

Mile 4 The road curves to the left; no chance of going wrong. Then it tops out over a low rise and runs straight across the flat plains of **Llano de La Paz.**

Mile 17 The village of **San Pedro** is strung out along the road. You can assuage your hunger at **Restaurant El Paraiso de San Pedro** (St. Peter's Paradise) on the right side. It's not fancy, but it's good.

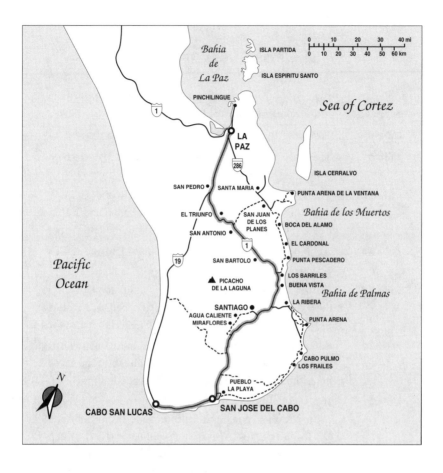

Mile 20   You come to a three-way intersection in the middle of not much. Mex 1 goes straight, while Mex 19 goes off to the right; they meet up again in Cabo San Lucas.

Mex 1 is now entering the **Sierra de la Laguna,** the mountain range that fills up most of the tip of Baja. The highest peak, **Picacho de la Laguna,** is over 7,000 feet tall; there's no road up there, as it is a natural reserve, but you can hike up. The Mountains of the Lake got their name because a lake used to exist south of the peak, although it ran dry a hundred or more years ago.

The asphalt is a delightful motorcycle road, full of twisty bits—which means you should take a good deal of care. A lot of four-wheeled wrecks can be seen along the way, decorating the *arroyos.*

The Road Less Traveled

This alternate route to Cabo has 30 miles of pavement followed by 30 miles of dirt road (XX). As the road runs south, town rapidly falls behind and you are, sooner than expected, in arid hills.

Mile 0   Turn onto BCS 286 from Mex 1 south of La Paz,

Mile 12   The **Cafe La Huerta** (Garden Cafe) offers good sustenance.

Mile 16   You crest the ridge on the **Sierra Novillo** and can look down on **Los Planes** (The Flats, The Plains) and **Bahia de la Ventana** (Window Bay) way off to the left.

Mile 24   At **Santa Maria,** a paved road runs off to the left to several fishing villages

Mile 26   Efforts have been made to improve a dirt road (XX) to the right, which runs up along a dry river bed for 15 miles to join with Mex 1 at a tiny village called **San Antonio.**

Mile 29   **San Juan de los Planes,** a small agricultural town of less than 2,000 people. Water deep beneath the ground irrigates the fruit, the veggies, and the thirsty cotton.

Mile 30   Just south of Los Planes the paved road turns left to head out to **Punta Arena de la Ventana** and a beautiful beach on **Bahia de los Muertos** (Deadmen's Bay). Keep straight; the dirt road (XX) is easy at first, and then plunges into some small mountains, the **Sierra el Carrizalito.** You have to get off the low mesa and zigzag down to the shore.

Once down low the graded road sticks to the coast, past **Boca del Alamo, El Cardonal,** and **Punta Pescadero,** places where *norteamericanos* are likely to be found building vacation homes. This area is known for its excellent fishing.

Mile 59   Pavement begins as you enter **Los Barriles.** Here you'll find **Hotel Playa del Sol** ($$$; phone U.S. 800-368-4334) and **Hotel Palmas de Cortez** ($$$; phone U.S. 800-368-4334) and **Tio Pablo's Restaurant,** open from 11:30 to 10 o'clock.

Mile 60   Rejoin Mex 1.

Mile 34   Entering **El Triunfo,** a splendid little mining town with lots of photogenic brick structures, even if it hasn't seen a working smelter for many a year. Silver was discovered in 1862, and gold soon after, and within 15 years the place had become a boomtown. Inevitably, the mines began to play out after the turn of the century, and by 1925 the place was down to a couple of hundred inhabitants.

The government likes to keep a bit of history intact in order to lure the tourist, and has since restored the old **Casa Municipal** (City Hall) along the main road. Close by, the **Restaurant Las Glorias** provides good Mexican fare.

"La Ramona" rises out of Kurt's helmet; when El Triunfo was a thriving mining center, the 140-foot smokestack, fired for the first time on St. Ramona's day, was the centerpiece of the town.

When you arrive at this rather ugly concrete ball by the side of Mex 1, you are 23 degrees, 27 minutes north of the equator, at the Tropic of Cancer.

If you turn at the little church, you can wind your way down several dirt roads to the huge brick smokestack, nick-named **La Ramona** because it was inaugurated on St. Ramona's day.

Mile 39 **San Antonio** is another old mining center which was founded back in the 18th century. It is now a small agricultural community with a small PEMEX down where the road curves around the dry river bed. Almost opposite the PEMEX is a dirt road that follows along the riverbed for 15 miles to **San Juan de los Planes.**

Mile 56 The village of **San Bartolo** is a little tropical haven, watered by a spring further up the canyon. Roadside stands sell mangos and avocadoes, and you can enjoy complete meals at any one of several restaurants in town. This is a common Sunday-drive destination for La Pazians.

Mile 64 The turn to the left to **Los Barriles** and **Bahia de Palmas.** Mex 1 now goes close to the seaside, with the hotels, RV camps, and fishing boats of the **Buena Vista** (Good View) area to your left. The road starts to climb again, the sea disappears, and soon you're back in the hills.

Mile 74 A paved road to the left goes seven miles to the village of **La Ribera** (see sidebar overleaf).

Mile 79 We're five miles beyond the La Ribera turn-off. A paved road on the right goes a mile or so to the town of **Santiago,**

founded back in 1723 with the building of the **Mission of St James the Apostle.** The road then crosses the **Arroyo de Santiago** and is usually covered with hard-packed sand. There is a PEMEX in the town center.

If you decide to take the dirt road (XX) you will come to a zoo—the only zoo, to my knowledge, in Baja. Being a claustrophobic type myself, I'm not much of a fan of zoos, preferring to meet my lions and bears in the wild. This **Jardin Zoologique,** however, is a pleasant place and is quite well maintained. Mostly it exhibits local fauna, from a mountain lion to peccaries and rattlesnakes. It also has an African lion and various monkeys. Admission is free, and the place seems to be open from morning 'til evening.

Mile 80   If you are interested in following dirt roads, keep going south beyond the zoo and you will pass through **Agua Caliente,** on to **Miraflores,** and back to Mex 1.

Mile 81   Here it is: at 23 degrees, 27 minutes north of the equator, you have just crossed into the **Tropic of Cancer.** The sun is directly overhead at noon during the Summer Solstice (and directly over the Tropic of Capricorn during the Winter Solstice). In fact, to define it astronomically, every point within "the tropics," (a/k/a The Torrid Zone) receives the perpendicular rays of the sun at least one day of the year. Unfortunately, this is not a very romantic spot, merely a scrubby pull-off by the side of the road, with a large graffiti-covered concrete ball to symbolize the earth.

Mile 87   At the PEMEX on the highway there's a paved road going right to the village of **Miraflores.** The place has a small, deserved reputation for making tack (the gear used for riding horses) as well as the more touristy stuff. One tannery is on the road into town, with a small sign reading LEATHER SHOP.

Mile 98   A sign on the road reads RAMAL LAS NARANJAS. This 32-mile dirt road (XXX) to the west leads over the **Sierra de la Laguna** and down to Mex 19 on the west coast. The first five miles are well-groomed, flat, and straight, and then the road starts the climb into the mountains. The next ten miles are quite good, going past a large citrus farm and several small ranches, but as it crests, the road deteriorates drastically, and may be impassable near the top. If the authorities have graded

The constant wind out on the East Cape distorted this wild fig tree
near Los Frailes.

Cabo del Este

The dirt road (XX) from La Ribera makes for a rollicking good excursion around the **Cabo del Este** (East Cape).

Mile 0   Turn off Mex 1 and head toward La Ribera (The Shore).

Mile 7   The pavement forks. The left fork heads straight into La Ribera. You want the right fork.

Mile 17   Come over a slight rise and down a shallow grade, and the pavement ends—just like that. The dirt road immediately starts to twist around as it gets down closer to the sea. This is the **Old Coastal Road.** For years the authorities have been planning on paving the entire stretch around **East Cape** and down to San Jose del Cabo; don't hold your breath. The dirt road, some 40 miles, is very well marked, and one would have to work hard to take a wrong turn.

Mile 18   A dirt road (XX) cuts back sharply to the left, the old road up the coast to Punta Arena and back to La Ribera.

. . . Continued . . .

Mile 24   A half dozen dusty miles and you are in the village of **Cabo Pulmo,** now dedicated to wind-surfing. You can rent an entire house for $50 and eat at **Chicago Nancy's Restaurant,** where Sylvestro the Chef turns out good dishes which can be geared to the American palate . . . "You want *picante* or no?"

Mile 29   For the lap of luxury you can stay at **Hotel Bahia Los Frailes** ($$$; (114) 10122; U.S. 800-762-BAJA) where you can go surfing and diving all day long, then swill margaritas and martinis in the evening. Even though it's in the middle of roughly nowhere, it is a full-service hotel, with a daily room-rate that includes three meals.

The next 20 miles are delightfully desolate, with the sea on your left, an occasional *rancho,* and the odd washout which needs to be negotiated with care.

Mile 31   A road goes off to the right, an alternative, more inland way back to Mex 1.

Mile 42   You come to the beginning of a build-up of huge houses belonging to rich people who live elsewhere. I'm just envious.

Mile 57   Come down a hill into the calm and quiet village of **Pueblo La Playa,** across the **Rio San Jose** from San Jose del Cabo. Pass the **Restaurant Los Dos Ricardos,** which is usually full of patrons, both Mexican and American. Head for the beach to find the **Hotel La Playita** ($$), with a detached restaurant where the chef is happy to cook up any fish you catch. Boats can be rented on the beach.

The road crosses the wide river mouth and comes into **San Jose del Cabo.** If you don't wish to wander about San Jose, take a left on the paved, divided, Boulevard Mijares, go down to where it T-bones into the seaside Boulevard Costera, and take a right. The road will meet up with Mex 1 after about a mile.

the western section you may be able to get through. Kurt has been all the way in years past, but I got buffaloed by a bad stretch at the top in 1996 and had to turn back. Hurricane Faustus whipped through there later that year, so I'm guessing that the pass is presently in poor shape, but the ride up is beautiful.

Mile 105   The busy **Los Cabos International Airport** is to your right. The highway becomes four lanes as it skirts **San Jose del Cabo.**

Mile 111   A paved road angles off to the left, past a PEMEX. This is the northerly approach to San Jose, along Calle Zaragoza. Do head into town—you'll get lost and have a good time (see sidebar next page).

Back on Mex 1, we are sweeping by San Jose, past the turn to the **Howard Johnson Hotel** and **golf course,** ($$$; phone (114) 20999; U.S. 800-524-5104) and down to the sea. Now you begin **The Corridor,** 18 glorious miles dedicated to The Tourist; this four-lane highway was completed in 1993, was immediately washed out by a hurricane, and was just as quickly repaired.

Mile 113   The turn to ZONA DE HOTELES and the Paseo Malecon San Jose.

Mile 114   The turn toward the condominiums of La Jolla de Los Cabos will put you on a short dirt road (XX) to **Playa Costa Azul** and the pseudo-surfer hangout of **Zippers.** Years ago it was a spot where the serious wave-catchers gathered to discuss the weather, but in recent years a lot of wannabees have moved in.

The next 12 miles of Mex 1 pass a series of resort hotels and a large PEMEX station on the land side.

Mile 115   The turn to **Hotel Palmilla** ($$$; phone (114) 20582; U.S. 800-637-2226), my favorite amongst the slew of expensive resorts along the coast. This one was built in 1956, when Cabo tourism was still in its infancy, and is pleasantly old-fashioned and pricey. Cobbled drives and lots of palm trees welcome you.

Mile 117   The antithesis of the Palmilla is the **Hotel Westin Regina Resort Los Cabos** ($$$; phone (114) 29000; U.S. 800-228-

A Real Mexican Town

San Jose is a real town, established by the Spanish in 1730 because it had a good source of water; it presently has 16,000 or so inhabitants. Half of the place is a genuinely Mexican town, the other half, mostly down on the coast, is dedicated to gently separating tourists from their money.

Calle Zaragosa bends a couple of times, taking you right downtown, past the church of San Jose and the *zocalo,* where the locals tend to hang out. The twin-steepled church was built in 1940 on the site of the 1730 **mission.** Over the doors is a mural portraying the killing of Padre Tamaral in 1734. Tamaral had the temerity to declare the local Indian custom of polygamy illegal; such high-handedness irritated the locals, so they sacked both this and the mission at Santiago. It reminds me of our battles with the Mormons over that same subject.

You can find the low-key tourism if you take a right turn onto the divided Boulevard Mijares. Mijares, to alert the politically correct types, was named for Lt. Jose Antonio Mijares, who died here fighting against the Americans in 1847.

The **Tropicana Inn** ($$; phone (114) 21580) on Blvd. Mijares has a sidewalk cafe where lots of people hang out; it's very nice, and as *gringo* as the town gets. On the north end of Mijares, close to the *zocalo,* is the city hall, with a collection of art and artifacts in the courtyard.

A favored eatery, the **Ristorante Damiana,** is on the northeast corner of the *zocalo.* South along Mijares, in a corner of a big empty lot where fairs are held, you'll find **Mariscos El Muelle,** an outdoor place which is open early in the morning until late a night.

Down on the shore, along the Paseo Malecon San Jose, a/k/a Boulevard Costera, you'll find the fancy hotels: **El Presidente** ($$$; phone (114) 20211; U.S. 800-327-0200), **Hotel Best Western Posada Real** ($$$; phone (114) 20155; U.S. 800-528-1234), the **Hotel Aguamarina** ($$; phone (114) 20701; U.S. 800-897-5700), and the **Fiesta Inn** ($$$; phone (114) 20793; U.S. 800-343-7821).

3000), a huge, pink, modernistic structure with 240 rooms high above the sea. This joint reputedly cost $200 million to build.

Mile 119 The **Hotel Melia Cabo Real** ($$$; phone (114) 30967; U.S. 800-336-3542) has a golf course and almost 300 ocean-view rooms built in a U shape. It has a vaguely Las Vegas air, as the lobby is done in the form of a pyramid.

Mile 121 The **Hotel Palacio de los Cabos** ($$$; phone (114) 33377) is next. With only 40 rooms, it's not quite as Grand Luxe as its neighbors.

Mile 122 A suitably ugly monument in the middle of the road commemorates the completion of the highway in 1993.

Mile 123 The vaguely Hawaiian-flavored **Hotel Cabo San Lucas** ($$$; phone (114) 33457; U.S. 800-733-2226), with 125 rooms, dates back to the late 1950s.

Mile 125 The **Hotel Twin Dolphin** ($$$; phone (114) 30496; U.S. 800-421-8925) was also built back in the 1950s, and since the number of tourists was far fewer in those years, it made do with only 50 rooms.

Mile 126 The **Cabo del Sol Resort** ($$$; projected to open in 1997, but you never know about these things), the latest, and possibly last, super deluxe hotel to be built along The Corridor. What a thing for me to say! Of course there will be more development.

Mile 132 The alternate road to La Paz via **Todos Santos** is Mex 19, which goes off to the right (see Chapter 19).

Mile 133 Kentucky Fried Chicken, Domino's Pizza, a condo salesman on every corner, the Giggling Marlin—**Cabo San Lucas,** we have arrived!

Cityscape Cabo San Lucas

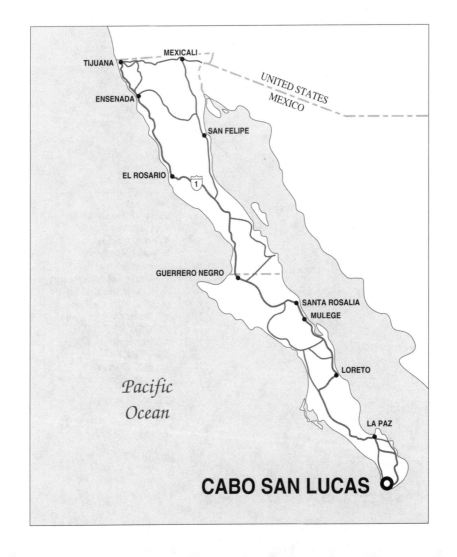

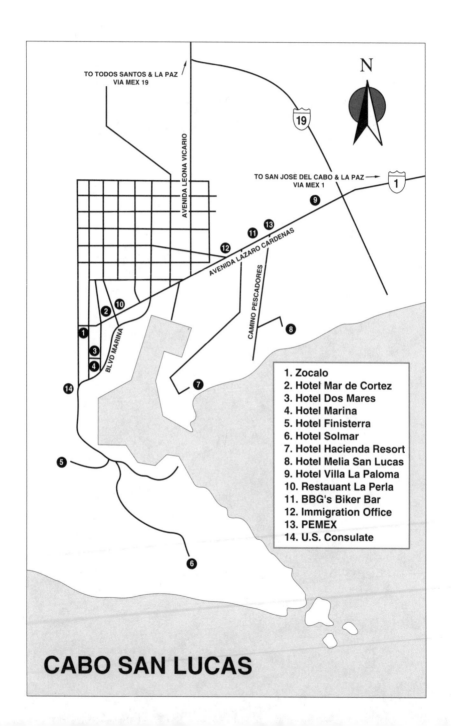

TO TODOS SANTOS & LA PAZ
VIA MEX 19

N

19

AVENIDA LEONA VICARIO

TO SAN JOSE DEL CABO & LA PAZ
VIA MEX 1

1

9

AVENIDA LÁZARO CÁRDENAS

CAMINO PESCADORES

13

11

12

2   10

1

8

3

BLVD MARINA

4

14

7

1. Zocalo
2. Hotel Mar de Cortez
3. Hotel Dos Mares
4. Hotel Marina
5. Hotel Finisterra
6. Hotel Solmar
7. Hotel Hacienda Resort
8. Hotel Melia San Lucas
9. Hotel Villa La Paloma
10. Restaurant La Perla
11. BBG's Biker Bar
12. Immigration Office
13. PEMEX
14. U.S. Consulate

5

6

CABO SAN LUCAS

18 Little Sin, Lots of Booze

There's no point in getting too detailed about this place; you should go and discover things for yourself. And the "essential" Cabo San Lucas is not all that big, though it has grown to a moderate size due to its vacation destination status. What I'll point out in this chapter are the high points and main features of Cabo, and you can fill in all the little details as you go around. Remember, the only reason for Cabo's existence is that it is one great big tourist mecca striving to please you.

In 1975, a big ferry boat coming up from **Puerto Vallarta** slid into the Cabo harbor, sidled up to the new concrete dock, and off-loaded a couple of dozen motorhomes and tourist cars, a few trucks, and a couple of motorcycles belonging to me and Ken, my longtime traveling friend (we were coming up from Panama following a two-year round the world trip—but that's another story). Cabo San Lucas had a few shops, a couple of resort hotels along the coast, two or three small hotels, and a couple of roadside stands selling souvenirs. That was it.

Several fishing boats decorate the Cabo harbor, but the hotel, marina, and shopping center in the background are much more profitable.

*Squid Roe is just
one of many,
many cheerful
bars in Cabo
San Lucas.*

(The ferry service to and from Puerto Vallarta was a great way to get deep into Mexico, but it was discontinued in 1989.)

Now Cabo is a minor city approaching 20,000 inhabitants, with tourist facilities to house another few thousand. The whole Cabo Corridor, the 20 miles from Hotel El Presidente in San Jose del Cabo to the Hotel Finisterra (Land's End) in Cabo San Lucas, can comfortably bed down some 10,000 tourists in more than 4,000 rooms.

Rolling into Cabo is easy: Mex 1 doubles as Avenida Lazaro Cardenas and feeds you right past the PEMEX station, and past IMMIGRACIONES (should you develop trouble with your tourist card).

You will go past **BBG's Biker Bar** on your right, a pleasant spot where you are welcome to park the bike right by the door. BBG's is not yet world-famous, although the owners would like it to be; they are trying in their own small way to take advantage of the Harley phenomenon.

Next you will go by **Latitude 22+** (a noisy bar), and past **Squid Roe** (more noise). Turn left just after Squid Roe and pick up Boulevard Marina, which runs alongside the marina, past **Carlos & Charlie's** (noise), and down to the **Giggling Marlin,** where, if you get drunk enough, you can have your feet tied and be hoisted up by block and tackle until you hang upside-down like a freshly caught tuna

Action city.

If you continue on, you will get to the quieter **Land's End** and **Playa Solamar.** If you follow Lazaro Cardenas, you will end up in the older part of town, dead-ending at Calle Cabo San Lucas and the *zocalo* (town square).

Cabo San Lucas is built around the old harbor. The general rowdiness hovers around the north side, while east and west the prices go up and the sounds go down. There are actually a couple of commercial fishing boats in the harbor, but I think it's more for the ambiance than for any real profit. If you own a boat and want to make serious money, you hire out to *gringo* fishermen.

Opposite that aforementioned PEMEX is Camino Pescadores, which goes down to **Playa El Madano** on the east side of the harbor. Most of Cabo around the old fishing port

Pizza Hut is one of several American-based fast-food outlets in Cabo, and Honda has the delivery-bike franchise.

and marina is on the noisy side; it was built up from a tiny fishing community to a serious Party Town. Life goes on until 2 or 3 a.m., and doesn't really get under way until about 11 o'clock the following morning. Minor-league dissipation and mild decadence is the way of life.

If you want to go big bucks, stay at the **Finisterra** ($$$; phone (114) 30100; fax 30590; U.S. 800-347-2252), built in 1968 and located off Marina Blvd. on Playa Solmar next to the U.S. Consulate—a bit far to walk into town. Even farther out on the peninsula near Land's End is the very upscale **Hotel Solmar** ($$$; phone (114) 33535; fax 30410; U.S. 800-878-4115). On the east side of the harbor, at Playa El Mendano, the **Hacienda Beach Resort** ($$$; phone (114) 30122; fax 30666; U.S. 800-733-2226) is reasonably gracious. Also aspiring to graciousness is the **Hotel Melia San Lucas** ($$$; phone (114) 34444; fax 30420; U.S. 310-410-1024), a bit farther along the beach.

If you want to stay in the thick of the action, you'll find any number of less pricey hotels on the smaller streets. I'm partial to the **Hotel Mar de Cortez Best Western** ($$; phone (114) 30032; U.S. 800-347-8821) with 70 rooms and a small pool. It's located two blocks before the *zocalo* on Lazaro Cardenas and is within walking distance to everything. Right on Boulevard Marina is the **Hotel Marina** ($$; phone (114) 32484). A low-bucks option is the **Hotel Dos Mares** on Calle Zapata ($$; phone (114) 30330), with a courtyard and tiny pool.

Food is all over the place, from U.S. chains like **KFC** and **Domino's** to semi-rarified dining experiences like **Mi Casa** on Calle Cabo San Lucas at the *zocalo*. This is probably the nicest place to spend your money, with half-indoor, half-outdoor dining, very handsome muraled surroundings, and good food. **Casa San Rafael,** the dining room of a small hotel on **Plaza Bonita** at the north end of the harbor, offers Mexico's version of *nouvelle cuisine* (new cooking); the ambience is elegant, the food excellent. And, on Camino Real you will find **Pavo Real,** a dinner-only place open from 6:00 to 10:00 which offers *haute cuisine* with a mixture of European and Mexican dishes.

How picturesque! Land's End framed by an adobe window.

La Perla on Lazaro Cardenas at Guerrero, gets my money for best local fare. However, to eat like a local, stop in at **El Pollo de Oro** on Lazaro Cardenas; five bucks gets you a whole lot of spit-broiled chicken, or ribs, or both.

Should you need the authority of the Government of the United States of America, the **U.S. Consulate** (phone (114) 33566) is located on Blvd. Marina at Pedregal, a block up from Hotel Marina on the west side of the harbor. Regular hours are Monday through Friday 10:00 to 1:00. If you have a genuine emergency during off-hours, the answering service will notify the consul. Remember, the consul is there to assist U.S. citizens in dire need, should you have an accident or get arrested, but is not going to help you if you have simply done something stupid like spend all your money.

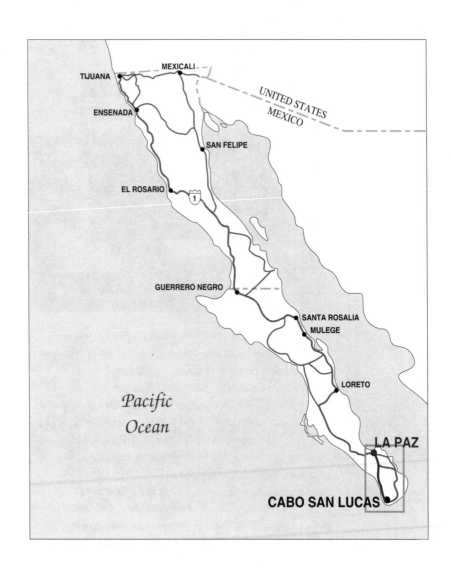

TIJUANA

MEXICALI

ENSENADA

SAN FELIPE

EL ROSARIO

1

UNITED STATES
MEXICO

GUERRERO NEGRO

SANTA ROSALIA
MULEGE

LORETO

*Pacific
Ocean*

LA PAZ

CABO SAN LUCAS

19 The Alternate Way Back

Down at the tip of the Baja peninsula, you can make a full loop on good pavement, taking Mex 1 from La Paz down to Cabo and Mex 19 back up to meet with Mex 1 at San Pedro, 20 miles south of La Paz.

All I can say is that I got there a lot faster than the guy on the bicycle did.

Mex 19 Through Todos Santos

Distance	*78 miles*
Terrain	*Gentle hills rolling along the coast up to Todos Santos, and then a flat plain leading to the intersection with Mex 1.*
Highlights	*Todos Santos is a pleasant small town, where one can escape the rather frenzied atmosphere of Cabo.*

Mile 0   If you head out of Cabo on the main drag, the divided Lazaro Cardenas, you pass the **Hotel Villa la Paloma** ($$), on the corner of Ave. Lazaro Cardenas and Mex 19; this is a bit far to walk to town or the beaches, but it does have a pool with a swim-up bar. Just beyond is the left turn onto Mex 19, which bypasses Cabo to the east.

Those who have become savvy about the city might choose to head up the one-way Avenida Leona Vicario, which goes north off Lazaro Cardenas three blocks east of the park; that's the urban Mex 19.

Mile 1   The two 19s meet, the road bears right, and a big PEMEX sits on the corner. Mex 19 runs through the industrial side of Cabo, something FONATUR (the Mexican tourist commission) would prefer you not see. But, hey, that's part of life. A large low-cost development has been built by the government to give the Cabo workers a place to live.

Pay heed to these little crosses by the roadside; they commemorate those who died in action on the highway.

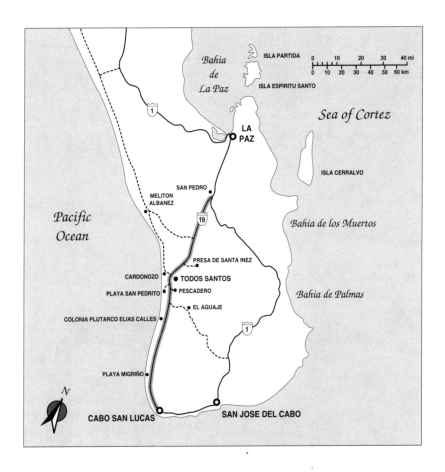

Mex 19 heads out of town at a rapid rate, climbing through sand and scrub without much traffic. Mex 19 was not paved until 1984, and while it is an easier, shorter route (by more than 30 miles) from La Paz to Cabo, people still don't use it often.

Mile 12   From up on the ridge and you can see the sea in front of you. This is a rocky, windy, cool coast, which so far has resisted serious efforts at development.

Mile 17   A dirt road (XX) goes down to **Playa Migriño,** a public beach which is usually empty.

Mile 30   The small agricultural community of **Colonia Plutarco Elias Calles,** also called **Rio Elias.**

With a palapa and a tent, life on Playa San Pedrito just south of
Todos Santos is good.

Mile 36 Turn on the dirt road (XX) to the right to get to **El Aguaje** and the road (XXX) over the **Sierra de la Laguna** (Chapter 17).

Mile 40 The village of **Pescadero** (pop. 1,200) is off to the right on a short bit of paved road. Roadside stands and **La Joya Loncheria** on the corner will provide food.

Mile 42 A reasonably good dirt road (XX) goes down to **San Pedrito RV Park & Restaurant,** which serves motorhome types and surfers.

Mile 44 To the left is a dirt road (XX) down to **Playa San Pedrito.** To the right are the botanical gardens of the **Campo Experimental Todos Santos,** with the best collection of Baja botany on the peninsula; visitors are welcome to look at the gardens during daylight hours.

Mile 46 Entering **Todos Santos** (All Saints), an agricultural oasis of some 5,000 inhabitants renowned for its tropical fruits; The area, called **Valle del Pilar** (Waterhole) sits right on the **Tropic of Cancer,** two miles from the sea. In 1723, the Jesuits founded a minor mission here, getting full **mission** status in 1733; it was then called **Santa Rosa de Todos Santos,** but the building has long since vanished.

Coming into town there is a PEMEX on the left, and then the sign that indicates Mex 19 takes a right turn. It does, but why miss the center of town? Continue straight. Pass the **Restaurant Santa Monica,** noted for its oysters. Turn right on the main street, Calle Juarez, and pass the ruins of the old sugar mill. The town was a sugar cane producer for a long time until the bottom dropped out of that market and the farmers diversified.

Halfway up Juarez is the small, old (1928) **Hotel California** ($$; phone (112) 40002), with **Restaurant Las Tejitas,** a bar, 16 rooms, and a tiny swimming pool. There are another half dozen small places to bed down, as the town is aspiring to becoming an **"artists' colony,"** which is always pleasant for a tourist.

Three blocks further, on the corner of Calles Juarez and Obregon is the **Casa de Cultura,** a small, eclectic **museum** covering history, geology, etc. It is open from 9:00 to 5:00 weekdays and 9:00 to 1:00 on Saturdays; donations are appreciated.

At the north end of town, two blocks up from the Hotel California, Calle Topete goes off to the left, turning into a dirt road (XX) that goes past the cultivated area of **Cardonozo,** and on to **Playa La Cachora.** From Cardonozo you can keep going north on dirt roads for a hundred miles along the coast, but beyond Meliton Albanez the road (XXX) can be tough going in sandy spots.

Mile 51   The dirt road (XX) to the right goes to **Presa de Santa Inez** (*presa* means dam) five miles away. The dam, completed in 1983, secured a steady water supply for Todos Santos.

Mile 62   The dirt road (XX) to the left catches the coast road (XXX) at **Meliton Albanez.** Mex 19 is comes out on the plain of **Llano de la Paz** and the road is straight and flat.

Mile 78   Junction with Mex 1 near the village of **San Pedro.**

The Hotel California in Todos Santos, built circa 1928, is an old-fashioned and pleasant place to stay.

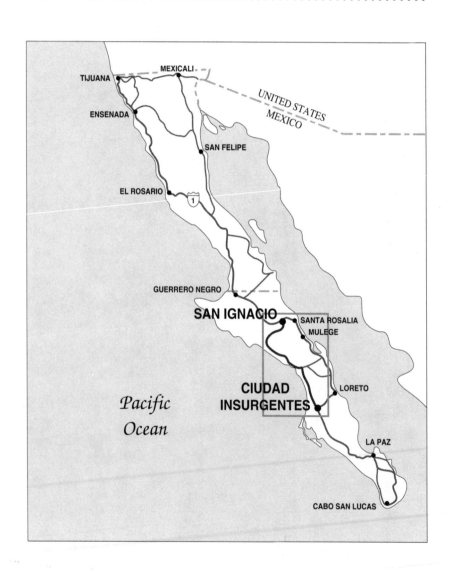

20 Taking the Old Road

. . . .

After the first 64 miles, this is mainly a dirt road—but it's one of the best rides in Baja for anyone on a dual-purpose bike.

Before the new paved Mex 1 crossed over the peninsula from to the Sea of Cortez and back over through the Sierra de la Giganta to Ciudad Insurgentes, truck traffic coming down the length of Baja would stay on the west side, the Pacific side, rumbling along slowly over the bad dirt roads. Hence the American nickname, **West Side Highway.**

I'll run you north because that is easier. Most riders will circle around via the Sea of Cortez and come back north this way. Also, should you decide that 141 miles of dirt road is too much rough stuff for your liking, you can hook over from La Purisima to Mex 1 south of Mulege on a mere 35 miles of good, hard, albeit unpaved surface (see Chapter 17).

Watch out on those water crossings!

To San Ignacio via the West Side Hwy

....

Distance   *206 miles*

Terrain   *From Ciudad Insurgentes you ride straight through the coastal plain to La Purisima, then head along a good dirt road that curves around the small hills leading up to Bahia San Juanico. As you proceed north, the flat country becomes cut by arroyos before reaching El Deleadito and the hardpan behind the Pacific beaches. From Laguna San Ignacio a good, but bumpy, dirt road leads into San Ignacio.*

Highlights *Enjoy dinner and a night in one of the palapas at the Scorpion Bay Campground (bring your own sleeping bag). The 50-mile trip up on the backside of the beach is my personal favorite stretch of Baja—it is just you and nobody else—and all within a day's ride from San Diego.*

Mile 0   Coming from the south from **La Paz,** Mex 1 makes a right angle by a little triangular park. You want to go straight, due north through **Ciudad Insurgentes.**

   You will find PEMEX on the left side of the highway as you enter the town.

Mile 1.5   The turn-off to the left to **Puerto Lopez Mateos.**

Sidetrip   Lopez Mateos Port is an advisedly quaint place, which some people have likened to the set in the Popeye movie of a few years back. Twenty miles of straight paved road gets you there. The town consists of a hundred or so houses, a small canning factory with a wooden pier where the boats pull up (that's the Popeye view), and a very basic hotel called the **Posada Ballena Lopez** ($$; no phone), which caters to affluent whale-watchers. A string of barrier islands runs down the coast for about 100 miles, and the **grey whales** often like to take these calm in-shore waters on their way south.

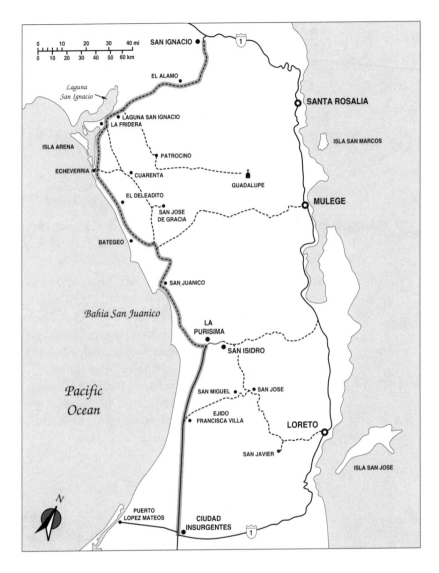

The West Side Highway goes straight north for 60 rather uninteresting miles, until you rise slowly and then come around a bend on the hill and see the wide mouth of the **Arroyo de la Purisima** down below you; the Pacific Ocean is off to your left.

Mile 64   At the bottom of the hill is a well-marked dirt road (XX) to the left going to San Juanico. However, roll on along the pavement and into **La Purisima** and fill up from the 55-gallon drums at the general store. I promise you, with just a couple of hundred inhabitants, and one street posing as the main one, you won't miss it.

Back out at the San Juanico turn-off, the road (XX) crosses the *arroyo* and climbs up the far side, winding around the side of the mesa, coming out on top. It is a well-maintained road, but you may encounter half-mile stretches of blown sand several inches deep, and that can put the wobblies in your stomach. After 20 miles you are looking out over the **Bahia San Juanico,** known to surfers the world over as **Scorpion Bay.**

Mile 93   Fishing boats will probably be pulled up on the beach, with some trucks loading the catch. You can go out and do a five-mile dash along the hard-packed sand near the water.

Mile 94   Up on the bluff is the little town of **San Juanico,** with the necessary amenities plus an airstrip. A little cantina on your left has food and drinks, and two doors up a workshop sells gas out of drums. If you want to spend the night—and you should—bring a sleeping bag and head half a mile west to the **Scorpion Bay Campground** on the bluffs (see sidebar).

Leaving San Juanico, the road north, the **West Side Highway,** is well defined. Nowadays it is little used except by locals and the occasional explorative *gringo*—and surf-

The West Side Highway has got one hellacious straightaway!

What More Do You Need?

The exceptional campground at Scorpion Bay offers several screened *palapa* huts in which to stay ($10 a person, bring your own bedding). Renting a *palapa* also gives you access to a very comfortable bathroom with hot water pouring out of the shower. The owner, Jaime Adkins, first came down here from San Diego in the 1960s with his father, and a few years ago decided to get out of the construction business. He is slowly building up his Scorpion Bay enterprise with an open-sided bar and a restaurant with excellent food.

The surfers can be found camping on the cliffs looking toward the west. Old-fashioned wave-running and new-fangled computers have married happily, and a serious enthusiast can plug into the Internet and find out about conditions just about anywhere. About ten California surfers were there the last time I was. They had heard in Los Angeles of a swell rising out of the waters off New Zealand, 6,000 miles away, which would eventually arrive at Scorpion Bay. They had packed up and driven 600 miles south, including a lot of dirt road, just to be here for the occasion. That's Jaime's major clientele, but he also knows several dirt-riding motorcyclists who want to set up a base at San Juanico, and maybe do fly'n'ride trips in the Sierra Guadalupe. It'd be a great idea!   ■

ers dashing down to Scorpion Bay in a beat-up pickup truck or Mummy's new Explorer. Little does Mummy know . . .

Mile 103   The road drops down into **Arroyo Santa Catarina,** where a small government road-maintenance outfit is based. There is usually some water in the creek, and you will splash through a rocky ford.

Mile 109   Here is the west end of the **Raymundo Road** (Chapter 14), which connects back to **Mulege.**

Mile 114   A big sign indicates the Low Road to **El Deleadito** to the left; the High Road, to **San Jose de Gracia,** is straight ahead.

The **Low Road** (XX) is my choice, as it travels on the salt pans behind the beaches, 50 miles of relative remoteness. Truckers in days of yore (pre-1973) loved it, as it

Sidetrip   The **High Road** (XXX) is ten miles shorter, but both
rougher going and less entrancing. The road is quite
good as far as San Jose, and then becomes more of a
struggle as you go north. Just beyond the hamlet of
Cuarenta a rough eight-mile connector off to the left
goes down to the beach. Keep straight, through some
longish stretches of soft sand along the way, and then
ride along the flank of the **Mesa La Salina.** After 42
miles, the road T's into the San Ignacio road near the fish
camp of **La Fridera.**

gave them some smooth going. Dropping off the mesa and
down to **Bategeo,** you pass a small goat ranch, and then
start whacking through some small dunes.

Mile 122   Keep to the right at the narrow fork; the left just deadends out
at another small ranch. One thing to keep in mind: despite the
casually made road you are following, and the occasional
bifurcation, you can rarely make a grievous error here. If you
do a wrong-turn to the left, the sea will fetch you up short in
a jiffy. The roads here change from season to season with
passing storms, but the main track is usually well-defined.
There can be some frantic run-off when it rains, water pour-
ing from the 6,500-foot level in the mountains down to the

*Life is very good
on the back
roads of Baja!*

The village store at El Deleadito is the only hot spot in 50 miles of beach travel on the West Side Highway.

beach in less than 15 miles. Do not try the Low Road just after a major storm, please.

Getting through the dunes means short stretches of soft sand, with a hard base anywhere from three to six inches down. However, once you are through the dune-ish stretch, about a mile all told, you are out on the flats, and the going is fast. Follow the tire tracks to keep from getting lost.

Mile 142   The fishing camp of **El Deleadito,** also known as **El Dalito,** is a lovely slum stretching along the beach for a half a mile. It grows as the years ago by; most of the people live up in San Jose and come down here seasonally when the catch is good. The *tienda* sells cold sodas (lots of ice around to keep the fish fresh). And you will be the talk of the town, and the focus of attention of everybody who is not working.

Mile 149   The road goes three ways, more or less, over the space of half a mile. The sharp turn to the right climbs over a dune and struggles up to the High Road. The left road goes across a small dike on a solar salt pond to deadend in the ramshackle village of **Echeverria.** If you want to see an endless expanse of pristine beach, turn left after going over the dike and the road will run you to the ocean.

What you want is that well-traveled middle road across the flats, sometimes going around sandy dunes, sometimes through them.

Mile 168   The end result is a series of small fish camps, including **La Fridera** on the shore of **Laguna San Ignacio.**

Mile 169   The intersection with the High Road, and the beginning of a long, bumpy ride up to San Ignacio. Pass through the fish camp of **Laguna San Ignacio.**

Mile 176   A road (XXX) goes off to the right to **El Patracino,** which Kurt says eventually connects with the road by the **Guadalupe Mission** . . . though this trek is not for the faint of heart. The road beyond El Patracino, not even shown on most maps, may see as much as one vehicle a week in the busy season. It is way out in the middle of the mountains with only a couple of very isolated ranches along the way, and if it gets washed out by a storm, it stays washed out for a while.

Mile 193   A little store at **El Alamo** (it means The Cottonwood Tree, in case you've ever wondered) has cold sodas. And then it is over the hill and down into **San Ignacio.**

Mile 206   You pass **Restaurant Tota** (Chapter 14) and are in the town. This little West Side Highway Jaunt rates high on my list of **"Memorable Rides."** It is the perfect run for big dual-purpose machines. And that 50 miles of Low Road is something you don't find many places in North America.

Up Close and Personal

Those in the whale-watching world do think that the watching aspect is far better here than at Scammon's Lagoon. However, since it is 40 miles of bad road to get here from San Ignacio, you have to be a dedicated cetaceophile either to put up with the daily pounding or to camp out along the bay. From several fish camps along Laguna San Ignacio, licensed guides will take you out in boats to get up close and personal with the mother whales and their calves. If you wish to go whale watching, just ask one of the locals where to find a guide and a boat. Don't speak Spanish? Tap yourself on the chest, then point out to the *laguna,* and then circle thumb and forefinger in front of each eye—the viewer should catch on and point you in some direction where you can repeat the process.

■

Appendices

A1 Motorcycle Stuff

If your motorcycle is in good shape, you shouldn't need anything in the way of parts. Potential Baja problems might include a broken cable, a nut or screw vibrating loose and falling out, or the bike falling over in just the wrong place and a rock punching a hole in the primary case.

Do not skimp on tires. Do not do one of those, "Ah, it has some miles left—it'll get me there and back and I'll change it when I get home." Put new rubber on before you leave.

I carry the basic tools that came with the bike, a tire repair kit, a few fix-it oddments, and a siphon.

The **tools** are just there to make you feel better. You are not going to strip down your DOHC, liquid-cooled engine and replace the crankshaft bearings in mid-trip. The wrenches and screwdrivers are in case nuts, bolts, or screws loosen up.

Having the tools for **tire repair** is a bit more essential. You can pick up a nail anywhere; it doesn't matter if you are in Mt. Vernon, Illinois, or ten miles north of La Pocitas, BCS. Know how to use your tire repair kit, whether plugging a tubeless tire or patching a tube. If I am on tube-type tires, I carry a spare rear tube with me. Have a suitable means of reinflating the tire; those CO_2 cartridge devices are nice, but a little bicycle pump is a good back-up. Every third business in Baja seems to be a *llantera* (tire repair shop), and you just might be lucky and find one at hand. Check your tire pressure regularly.

My **fix-it stuff** usually includes some duct tape, a tube of JB Weld, and a pair or two—different sizes—of self-locking pliers (a/k/a Vise-Grips). It is amazing what can be accomplished with this when you have some ingenuity and no other choice: imagine that the bolt securing your shift lever loosens up and the lever falls off somewhere along the road; Vise-Grips will let you shift gears in such a pinch.

If you are riding a dual-purpose bike with a chain, I'd advise your carrying a spare links and a chain-breaker. I have known of riders patching a broken chain together with a bit a wire so they could limp to the nearest salvation, but that won't work very well if you have any big hills to climb. On chain-driven street bikes, I make sure that the chain and sprockets are in good shape before I leave. The technology in modern chains is so good you'll be hard put to bust one unless you let it get completely out of adjustment, or something gets stuck between the chain and the sprocket.

If you are paranoid, you might bring along extra throttle and clutch cables.

The most common failures in street bikes in Baja often occur in the electrical systems, when a wire simply shakes loose. Carrying a couple of spare fuses is not a bad idea—but take the time to figure out why the first fuse blew before you install the second one and blow that one, too.

A **siphon** is just a general, practical thing to have, especially if you are going down some of the dirt roads, and might have to replenish your gasoline supply from a passing pickup.

I presume things won't go wrong, and all I have suffered over the years is a couple of flat tires. After stating this, being a mildly superstitious fellow, I have just knocked on wood.

A2 Food, Water, & Health

If you are going to hang out at the tourist zones, you won't have to eat anything that your Nebraska grandmother wouldn't have been proud to prepare for you.

But that is not the purpose of traveling. Get a bit daring. Try some *menudo* (tripe stew). Have some *pulpo al mojo de ajo* (octopus in garlic sauce). My theory about food is that if the locals eat and enjoy it, it is good. It might require a drastic alteration to my gastronomic sensibility, but that's part of the pleasure.

Any hotel restaurant catering to the traveler will be happy to serve you up a slice of cooked cow adorned with French fried potatoes, but that's sort of missing the point of travel.

Seafood is good and plentiful the length of Baja, from the omnipresent *huachinango* (red snapper) to half a dozen varieties of sea bass. Often the word on the menu is the generic *pescado* (fish), and trying to define it further can be problematical. *Camarones* (shrimp) and *langosta* (lobster) are popular among tourists, and priced accordingly.

Breakfast, such as eggs scrambled with Mexican sausage *(huevos con chorizo),* can be eaten any time of day and comes with *refrijoles* (refried beans) and *tortillas,* often with a bit of lettuce and tomato on the side. I have no qualms about eating washed veggies, but I also understand the *norteamericano* fear that the water for the washing may not have been terribly clean.

The roadside stands *(loncherias)* are where I go for **lunch;** perhaps you run a minor risk of a severely upset stomach, but— no guts, no glory. Also, the woman running the place is not making her profit off of you, but off the locals who eat there consistently. Your lunch will bear very little resemblance to Taco Bell. A Baja *burrito* is usually a lot thinner than the *norteamericano* version. *Tacos* are soft *tortillas* wrapped around meat or fish. A *flauta,* usually three or four to a serving, is a *taco* wrapped around meat in a fluted manner and then deep-fried in oil. *Tamales* consist of ground corn filled with meat or veggies, wrapped in a corn husk and steamed. Don't be afraid to try.

A bottle of purified **water** should go in your saddlebag. Every *tienda* sells it in liter bottles for 20 cents or so. Out in the countryside I have drunk a lot of well water and never suffered—it is the tap water I tend to be leery of, except in the tourist hotels; they don't want you to be sick. However, the only time I have suffered the *turistas* was after staying in a tourist hotel over on the mainland.

Essentially, the **turistas** occur when little bugs that your system is accustomed to get into your intestines (Mexican visitors coming to the United States often suffer the "tourists," since they are used to different bugs than we have up here). Your body will eventually heal itself in a day or so, but in the meantime you can take a medicine like Imodium or Lomotil, which shuts down your undesirable intestinal urges until you regain natural control.

A small array of **first-aid** products is good to have along, with Band-Aids, antiseptic cream, anti-itch spray, tweezers (for picking out thorns), and some anti-*turistas* pills. I carry several large gauze pads and a long wrap-around bandage for larger chores.

Keep a good supply of **sun-block** on hand, and ride with your arms covered. The Baja sun can roast you if you are not careful.

Don't worry too much about **critters.** The worst I have come up against are flies and mosquitoes; I've never seen a snake down there in the wild, let alone a rattler, though they do exist.

Some people might say I am treating this whole matter of health much too lightly, but in truth, you are never more than one hellaciously long day from an American hospital in California. And, I think that if you are exceedingly cautious and only eat out of sealed containers, you will miss the very essence of a good trip to Baja. Basically, I eat anywhere the food looks good, am circumspect about the water, and carry a roll of toilet paper in the tankbag just in case I feel the need to stop along some remote stretch of road.

If anything, worry about avoiding a crash, although by buying this book you have symbolically sworn on a stack of Motorcycle Safety Foundation manuals that you will ride safely and responsibly while in Baja

If you get sick or are injured while in the northern Tourist Zone, I would head back over the border. Down south, the U.S. Consulate in Cabo (phone (114) 33566) can recommend doctors in the Tourist Zone and La Paz. And, any major tourist hotel will have a *medico* (doctor) on call. On the long stretch between Ensenada and La Paz, the larger towns have doctors, clinics, ambulance services, and airstrips for medical evacuation. If you don't want to be too far from your friendly HMO, you can contract with Air-Evac International (phone 800-254-2569), Critical Air-Medicine (phone 800-247-8325), or SOS Assistance (phone 800-523-8930) for insurance to cover your trip.

You should know that the most common illness affecting *gringos* in Baja is a hangover.

A3 Books on Baja

● ●

This little book is really all you need for a happy trip from TJ to Cabo. However, there are an awful lot of other books on Baja worth reading.

Thirty years ago, a researcher named Ellen Barrett published the *Baja California Bibliography,* (Bennett & Marshall), which listed more than 2,800 books and articles on the subject that were published between 1535 and 1964. I would imagine that another 500 have hit the presses since then.

If I were to take one **companion volume** to this book it would be Joe Cummings' *Baja Handbook* (Moon Publications), which covers the entire peninsula in detail. He has also done the *Cabo Handbook,* which focuses on the area between La Paz and the two Cabos in even greater detail. The advantage of such a book is that virtually every hotel, restaurant, and museum is included.

Many other Baja **guidebooks** exist, whether you're interested in culinary ratings, kayaking along the shore, seeing all the cave paintings, or knowing the best surf spots. Your friendly library or bookstore can run up a list of what's available. The Discover Baja Travel Club (3089 Clairemont Dr., San Diego, CA 92117; U.S. phone 800-727-2252) has a list of 60 current books on the subject.

It is easy to overload yourself, but much of the reading is great fun. Graham Mackintosh wrote *Into A Desert Place,* about the 3,000-mile hike he took around the peninsula in the early 1990s—a trip I would not care to make. At the other end of the literary spectrum, Gene Kira recently published a novel, *King Of The Moon,* about fishing life on the Sea of Cortez.

The more you know about this place, the better time you will have. Knowing about Baja will also involve a decent map or two. The best **roadmap** of Baja California that I know of is put out by AAA, in its local guise as the Auto-mobile Club of Southern California. Its scale is about 1:800,000, and it is detailed and accurate, even on the very back roads. It is worth joining the AAA just to get this map (phone 800-924-6141).

My second choice is the *Traveler's Reference Map of Mexico: Baja California,* put out by International Travel Map Productions (P.O. Box 2290, Vancouver, BC V6B 3W5, Canada). The scale is 1:1,000,000, and there is a bit of clutter, but the map is still quite usable; a second edition was done in 1992, but a third may be on its way.

If you really want to get serious with **topographic maps** down to 1:50,000, get in touch with MapLink (25 East Mason Street, Santa Barbara, CA 93101; 805-965-4402). They carry state maps of both Baja California (Norte) and Baja California Sur.

No need to get lost in the Baja.

A4 Some Words of Spanish

You don't need to speak Spanish to enjoy Baja, especially in the tourist zones, where English is widely spoken by the locals. It's polite, however, to know a few dozen Spanish words. These can be quite useful in that long stretch between Ensenada and La Paz. And traveling in foreign lands is a lot more fun when you speak at least a little of the language.

One thing to remember: if the person you are talking with does not understand your English, or your attempt at Spanish, talking louder won't help.

Unlike our own English language, Spanish pronunciation is consistent and nearly phonetic, and the basic elements of communication are easily acquired.

Alphabet The Spanish alphabet consists of 28 letters. Note that *k* and *w* are not part of the Spanish alphabet and only appear in words of foreign origin; the letters *ch, ll, ñ* and *rr* are counted as separate letters and even command their own separate sections in the dictionary.

Vowels You may not have noticed, but unstressed vowels in English all sound alike. This is not the case in Spanish, where vowels retain their own unique identities.

a sounds like *ah* in father

e most often sounds like *ay* in way

i most often sounds like *ee* in week

o sounds like *oh* in go

u most often sounds like *oo* in food, but takes on the characteristics of a *w* after consonants other than *q*

y sounds like Spanish *i* when standing alone or at the end of a word

Consonants Spanish consonants (for the simple purpose of making oneself understood) are virtually identical to English equivalents. If you want to get fancy, however, you can note the following distinctions:

b sounds like an English *b* at the begining of a word, or following the letter *m;* otherwise pronounce it without letting your lips touch

c sounds like an *s* before the letters *e* and *i,* otherwise it's like an English *k*

d sounds like the *th* in weather

g sounds like an English *h* before the letters *e* and *i,* otherwise it's like the *g* in go

h is always silent in Spanish

j resembles an English *h* with more force behind it

ñ sounds like the *ni* in onion

r is similar to the *dd* in ladder, except when it is at the beginning of a word, and then it is rrrrolled with Spanish flair. The combination of **rr** is always rolled.

v is indistingushable from Spanish *b* (see above)

x may sound like the *x* in taxi, but sometimes like a Spanish *j*

z sounds like the *s* in sun

Stress   *Muy facil.* Words ending in vowels or *n* or *s* have their accentuation on the next-to-last syllable. Words ending otherwise have their stress on the last syllable. Visible written accent marks (omitted in this text) override these two rules. Also, you'll notice the Spanish tone of voice remains very even during a converstion—very different from English, where individual words and ideas are emphasized apart from the other words in a given sentence.

Phrases   Once again, you really don't need to speak Spanish to make your way around Baja, especially in the tourist zones, but any attempt (no matter how feeble) will make for a richer experience. You'll want a generic phrase book for this purpose, but here are a few sentences for practice.

I don't speak much Spanish.
No hablo mucho español.
(noh AH-bloh MU-choh ays-PAH-nyol)

Speak slowly, please.
Hable despacio, por favor.
(AH-blay days-PAH-syo, por fah-VOR.)

Good morning/day.
Buenos dias.
(BWAY-nos DEE-ahs)

Good afternoon/early evening.
Buenos tardes.
(BWAY-nos TAR-days)

Good evening/night.
Buenos noches.
(BWAY-nos NO-chays)

Goodbye.
Adios. (literally, "to God")
(ah-DYOS)

Thank you.
Gracias.
(GRAH-syas)

How much?
¿Cuanto cuesta?
(KWAN-toh KWAYS-tah?)

How much for a room?
¿Cuanto cuesta para un cuarto?
(KWAN-toh KWAYS-tah PAH-rah oon KWAR-toh?)

Excuse me.
Perdoneme.
(pehr-DOH-nay-may)

Full (like at a gas station).
Lleno.
(YAY-noh)

Where is the Hotel Perla?
¿Donde esta el Hotel Perla?
(DOAN-day es-TAH el OH-tell PEHR-lah?)

Do you sell gas here?
¿Vende gasolina aqui?
(BEN-day gah-soh-LEE-nah ah-KEE?)

Is he a Harley mechanic?
¿Es un mecanico de Harley?
(ays oon may-CAH-nee-coh day AR-lee?)

It's leaking a lot of oil.
Esta tirando mucho aceite.
(ace-TAH tee-RAN-doh MOO-choh ah-SYAY-tay)

Can you fix it?
¿Lo puede arreglar?
(loh PWAY-day ah-rray-GLAR?)

Where is a telephone?
¿Donde esta una caseta de telefono?
(DOAN-day ays-TAH OON-ah cah-SAY-tah day tay-LAY-foh-noh?)

How far to La Paz?
¿Quantos kilometros a La Paz?
(KWAN-tohs kee-LOH-may-trohs ah lah pas?)

Show me the road to Tecate.
Enseneme el camino a Tecate.
(en-SEN-ay-may el cah-MEE-noh ah tay-KAH-tay)

Bathroom/toilet.
Baño.
(BAH-nyoh)

Toilet paper.
Papel higienico.
(pah-PELL ee-HYAY-nee-coh)

My motorcycle is very fast.
Mi moto es muy rapido.
(me MOH-toh ace mooey RAH-pee-doh)

Want to race?
¿Quiere participar en una carrera?
(KYER-ay par-TEE-see-par en OON-ah cah-RRAY-rah?)

¡Buena suerte! Good luck!

A5 Guided Tours to Baja

This book is intended for the rider who wants to go to Baja alone, or with some friends, and stick to the recognizable roads. In other words, it is for pavement pounders like me, with a few excursions down some good—and some not so good—dirt roads.

However, recognizing that not everyone might be happy with solo voyaging into darkest Baja, I will mention three motorcycle touring companies who have set up organized road tours in Baja, and include very brief descriptions of their routes. To find out more, contact the company.

These companies take care of everything, from paperwork to wake-up calls. However, even if you are having the whole trip laid on by one of these tour outfits, do take this book, as you will be able to flabbergast your co-riders by knowing more than even your guide about where you are going.

• **Pancho Villa Moto-Tours,** 685 Persimmon Hill, Bulverde TX 78163; phone 800-233-0564 or 830-438-7744; fax 830-438-7745.

Skip Mascorro, *jefe* of Pancho Villa Moto-Tours, knows his way around the Mexican neighborhoods, whether on the mainland or the peninsula. On his 16-day tour he'll meet you in Nogales, Arizona, and you can either provide your own motorcycle or Skip will arrange a rental. He runs the tour down the mainland side of the Sea of Cortez to Mazatlan, then ferries you over to La Paz. From there it is down to Cabo and back up the 1000 miles to Tijuana. Naturally a chase vehicle carries the luggage.

• **Von Theilmann Tours,** P.O. Box 87764, San Diego CA 92138; phone 619-463-7788.

Mike von T. has been in the motorcycle tour business a long, long time. Since his headquarters is in San Diego, it is easy for him to set up a great 12-day tour down to Cabo and back. He'll keep you on the pavement, if you wish, but those with a desire to try some of Baja's better dirt roads can veer off from the main group on occasion. Chase vehicle included. Rental bikes are available.

• **EagleRider Motorcycle Tours & Rentals,** (Harleys only) 20917 Western Ave., Torrance CA 90501; phone 310-320-4008; fax 320-4176.

EagleRider runs its 7- and 16-day Baja tours out of San Diego, going south to Cabo San Lucas. If you don't come with your own Harley, they will be happy to rent you one, from a Sportster to a Heritage Springer; I'll take the Road King myself, thank you. A guide and a vehicle carry the extra stuff letting you ride without a worry in the world—except do pay attention to the road.

In case you have been infatuated with all the reports of riding the Baja 1000, I will also include here three semi-off-road tour organizations who which be happy to take you around the peninsula on some rougher roads through the occasional desert and beach. They will make sure you don't get lost, have a place to stay, and will haul the gear. It's very simple: you give the outfit money, the outfit does everything else, from carrying your bags around to making sure the bike is in top shape.

These companies do vet their customers to make sure they have some sort of background in dirt riding. The rides are generally not difficult, but a rider who has never taken his Royal Star off the asphalt might find himself at a loss in soft dirt on a dual-purpose bike.

• **Baja Off Road Adventures,** 3950 East Miraloma, Anaheim CA 92806; phone 714-528-6539; fax 630-4474.

This company will set you up with a three- or four-day trip, taking in Mike's Sky Ranch and other remote places in northern Baja. BORA bosses Nick and Charlie Peltzer, who are long-time Baja buffs and have a house south of Ensenada, will pick you up at the San Diego airport, provide you with a Honda XR600, and show you lots of surprising sights.

• **Baja Off Road Tours**, 25108 Marguerite Parkway, #B-126, Mission Viejo CA 92692; phone 714-830-6569.

This outfit does longer trips: four day loops around northern Baja, or eight-day one-way trips all the way south to Cabo. The BORT boss, Chris Haines, has been a Baja 1000 competitor for many years, and was a winner in '87. He knows his stuff. You are picked up in San Diego, driven to Ensenada, provided with a Kawasaki (from a KX200 to a KLR650), and treated to a blast.

• **Embajador Adventure Tours,** 3368 Governor Drive, #F-246, San Diego CA 92122; phone 800-522-6483; fax 619-453-4958.

Embajador also does four- to eight-day tours, either in the high country of central northern Baja, or farther south. Todd Way and Tom Grady have been Baja-ing for 30 years, running EAT for the past five years, and know the roads. You'll have pickup in San Diego, a Honda XR600 at your disposal, and nothing else to worry about but staying upright.

Pavement or dirt, take your choice. But any way you get to see Baja is good.

Give a call, or drop a note in the mailbox, and you'll get the brochures to tell you more about these trips.

•••

An octagonal sign always means STOP

STOP

Triangular signs always mean CAUTION

WORKMEN   TOPES   SCHOOL
              (SPEED BUMPS)   CROSSING

Rectangular signs are INFORMATIONAL

NO LEFT TURN   ESCUELA

                PARKING   ONE HOUR PARKING   SCHOOL
            (ESTACIONAMIENTO)   (ESTACIONAMIENTO)

A6 Mexican Road Signs

Mexico is plugged into the international road sign symbols concept. Most signs are easy to interpret.

Children = School zone.

Guy with shovel = Construction zone.

Car on a downhill slope = Steep grade.

When you see a circle crossed by a bar, it means DON'T.

The most important thing to remember is that a diamond- or triangular-shaped sign means CAUTION or DANGER. So watch out, even if you don't understand what it says. The two signs that most *norteamericanos* might not be fully aware of, and should be, are those for *tope* (speed bump), and *vado* (dip).

Officially, Mexican traffic rules are pretty much like those in effect in the U.S.; unofficially, motoring is a bit different.

In crowded urban settings, such as Tijuana, might often makes right: at an intersection, don't debate the right of way with a large truck. A corrollary to the above rule states that the older vehicle has the right of way: the relaxed driver of the beat-up '72 Buick has a lot more going for him than the nervous nelly with the '97 Dodge.

Also, many Americans are not familiar with the etiquette of the *glorieta* (traffic circle): the car in the circle has the right of way.

On my relatively small motorcycle, I defer to anybody who wishes to challenge me, whether it is an elderly, sombreroed vaquero loafing along in a '62 Pinto, or a taxi driver eager to terrify his client with a wild ride to the airport.

Out in the countryside I am also deferential. If you come up behind a truck and a left turn signal goes on, it may mean that the road ahead is clear and he is inviting you to overtake him. Or, it could mean that the driver is turning left. It makes for interesting decision-making.

Never, ever presume that you can read the mind of the driver in front of you, whether traveling in your direction or coming toward you. I was once following a friend through a small village in the untrafficked countryside where the houses were set back about 30 feet from the asphalt. An aged sedan in front of us pulled off onto the dirt to the right. Just as my friend started to accelerate past, the sedan's driver began a sweeping U-turn. That was a close one!

The best advice I can offer is *be cautious,* and when in doubt speed up, slow down, stop, or get out of the way, depending . . .

If you really want to get into the semiotics of highway signing, I would recommend you buy Ed Culberson's *Road Sign Translator: Spanish to English* (Whitehorse Press, phone 800-531-1133). But the previous stuff should get you through Baja.

About the Author

Clement Salvadori graduated from a three-speed Raleigh bicycle to a friend's Harley 125 when he was 15. A year later he got his driver's license, bought an NSU 250, and acquired a taste for the open road, paved or not. After expending much time and money on a formal education, he made several attempts at pursuing conventional employment that did not directly involve motorcycles—although he did get the U.S. Department of State to assign him a Vespa as his official vehicle when working in Saigon. However, at the age of 33, he quit his last real job and proceeded to squander what savings he had on a two-year trip around the world on his BMW R75/5. When a motorcycle publication actually paid him money for a story he had written about riding to Afghanistan, he realized a whole new career was opening up.

Since then, he has earned a living of sorts by editing and writing for motorcycle magazines. He's a senior editor at both *Rider* and *American Rider.* He has also been a Baja aficionado since 1975 and goes down there several times a year. He lives in Atascadero, California, which he claims offers the best year-round riding in the world, only 300 miles from the Mexican border.

Index